Africa's Anthropological Dictionary on Love and Understanding:
Marriage and the Tensions of Belonging in Cameroon

Peter Ateh-Afac Fossungu

Langaa Research & Publishing CIG
Mankon, Bamenda

Publisher
Langaa RPCIG
Langaa Research & Publishing Common Initiative Group
P.O. Box 902 Mankon
Bamenda
North West Region
Cameroon
Langaagrp@gmail.com
www.langaa-rpcig.net

Distributed in and outside N. America by African Books Collective
orders@africanbookscollective.com
www.africanbookcollective.com

ISBN: 9956-791-05-9

© Peter Ateh-Afac Fossungu 2014

DISCLAIMER

Table of Contents

Synopsis

This book deals with love, marriage, and family issues generally but its central question remains that of whether love without understanding is love. Love and understanding could indeed be just what the world needs to be a better place for all of us. The duo (love and understanding) would also be the foundation of any successful marriage and/or family. Difficult and infrequent as it is to stumble on the duo, the book demonstrates how Momany seems to have been extremely blessed with often having the rare duo constantly waiting at his doorsteps. But the 99-Sense Theory (with its two ugly arms) has obviously been a constant and persistent obstacle to the speedy realization of his objectives. The 99-Sense Theory (or 99-Sensism) deals with the Bangwa people's popular epithet in Cameroon; the paradox in this whole affair being that Momany often suffers because of his 99-sensical appurtenance (outside arm) whereas behaviourally (by the inside arm) the man does not appear to be a 99-senser, but instead what the book calls 'a globavillagist'. The outside arm of 99-Sensism refers to the perception of the Bangwa by the non-Bangwa while the inside arm squarely deals with the comportment of the Bangwa themselves that leads the others to fear having serious dealings (like marriage and family) with them. This book's merit is not just limited to ethnic/cultural relations and (other) exclusion such as Momany's. It is most importantly worthy because it deals with love from much broader and interdisciplinary angles than just the love-making (and associated pleasures) that most love stories would seem to solely focus on. This book appears to be unique as it crucially raises and brings new and sometimes wholly ground-breaking perspectives on the subject-matters of love and understanding, of marriage, and of family. It will most likely leave many experts (from across many disciplines, continents and societies) with much to ponder about and do further theoretical and applied (evaluation) research on.

Introduction

Some of my reflections have focused on conversations within the CAE [Council on Anthropology and Education]. I have heard many colleagues express the view, in one form or another, that our field needs revitalization. In these discussions, colleagues have expressed differing opinions concerning our relationships with cultural anthropology and with educational research and practice. Some CAE members urge us to strengthen our connections with theory and research in cultural anthropology; others contend that we should strengthen our connections with practitioners. Often, these are treated as competing goals....

Although a particular study often is oriented *primarily* toward theory or practice for its source of questions and intended contributions, I do not see the focus on theory or practice as a dichotomy. To elaborate on the image presented above, I think it is useful to think of the "roads" intersecting in the CAE as two continua. One axis involves low to high theory orientation; the other involves low to high practice orientation. In this view, orientations to theory or practice are not oppositional, but are complementary dimensions, with the result that there can be varying combinations (for example, high theory to high practice orientation, high theory to low practice orientation, moderate theory to high practice orientation, and so on) [Jacob, 2001: 266-67].

Love and Understanding and the 99-Sense Theory at a Glance

An epithet is: (1) any <u>word</u> or phrase applied to a person or thing to describe an actual or attributed quality: *"Richard the Lion-Hearted" is an epithet of Richard I;* (2) a characterizing word or phrase firmly associated with a person or thing and often used in place of an actual <u>name</u>, title, or the like, as "man's best friend" for "dog"; (3) a word, phrase, or <u>expression</u> used invectively as a term of abuse or contempt, to express hostility, etc.[1] I will be returning later on in this Introduction to the concept but, for now, know that the third connotation is particularly useful to this book's main research question which, intricately tied to Cameroonian ethnic groups politics as it is, would demand the attention of anthropologists, among other social and/or behavioural scientists. According to some experts in the definitional field, anthropology is: (1) the science that deals with the origins, physical and cultural development, biological characteristics, and social customs and beliefs of humankind; (2) the study of human beings' similarity to and divergence from other animals; (3) the science of humans and their works; and (4) also called philosophical anthropology, it is the study of the nature and essence of humankind.[2]

Inviting Behavioural Scientists to Help

Science, according to Reaves (1992: 20), is one particular way of finding out about the world, and this includes the world of people, their actions and their feelings. The best way to understand this, Reaves concludes, is to look at what scientists try to do and the sorts of thinking they use along the way. Anthropology being one of the behavioural sciences, behavioural scientists,[3] Reaves (1992: 1) thinks, are interested in behaviour, primarily the behaviour of people; with there being many different sorts of behavioural scientists who are interested in the things people do, why they do them, and what we can learn by studying people and animals in many different situations. Love is obviously one of such 'many different situations' and Momany's narratives on love and understanding (while involving all of them) would lean mostly on the first and fourth significations of

---

[1] http://dictionary.reference.com/browse/epithet

[2] See http://dictionary.reference.com/browse/anthropology

[3] Not to be confused with, and limited to, those of them using or adhering to the behavioural approach or method and who are popularly known as behaviouralists. For more insights into behavioural analysis, see Sanders (2010).

anthropology given above, with love and understanding being the foci of and complements to humankind in them.

Admittedly, this writer is not an anthropologist, professionally speaking, and therefore is very unlike Weis and Fine (2013:223) who clearly "occupy what might be considered the position of 'outsider within,' as we are simultaneously both within and outside of the specific subdiscipline that lies at the epicenter of this paper [or book]." I do think however that I need not necessarily to be 'inside' or 'within' to be able to offer the insiders "empirical materials 'on the ground'" (Weis and Fine, *id*: 224) with which said experts could falsify their theories "in the clouds"; or to furnish them with Hancké's (2010: 236-37) 'research questions' to work on. Research, according to the experts (Reaves, 1992: 10 & 8; Gonzalez, 2001: 388), is a systematic way of generating and answering questions about the world. Some of such questions, for instance, that I am inviting the experts to keenly follow this discussion and look into could be: Is love without understanding really worth describing as love or just love-making or pretentiousness? Put in other words, can you really love someone and yet not understand him or her?

Of course, we can quickly point to there being love at first sight (and there is much of this type also in this book); but could that love be real and durable without mutual (knowledge of and) understanding engrafted upon it? Can it be said that what appears to be so hard to find is not someone for love-making; that it is rather *mulovundism* (mutual love and understanding) that would be difficult to find and maintain? *Mulovundism* obviously opposes *onsilovundism* (one-sided love and (mis)understanding). From the narratives of this book, love seems to be one of those domains where prior experience is not very essential for practising it excellently. Could this most probably be because love comes naturally, when real; and, therefore, often boldly seeking to transcend some artificial boundaries or restrictions? Do some of these issues not merit researching into by more erudite heads? Talking of research, love, again, is apparently an area where not much research appears to have been conducted outside love-making or sex. This book is coming, inter alia, to call on the behavioural and other scientists to refocus or resituate and correct this deficiency. The book also, as Stoker and Marsh (2010: 1) would want to say, "aims to provide an introduction to the way that ... [lovers or those in love] carry out their [strateg]ies"; the attainment of these objectives being greatly assisted, perhaps, by the experiences and preaching of people like Momany who would view sex as just a minuscule part of the expression of love;[4] instead putting the emphasis on understanding to the point of doubting if love without it is love.

Love and understanding could indeed be just what the world needs to be a better place for all of us. The love and understanding duo is capitally essential for a successful marital union and/or family – "the basic unit for raising children."[5] Hard and rare as it is to stumble on the duo, Momany would seem to have been extremely lucky in having them often dutifully laying (and even begging, I would say) at his *heart-steps* – or doorsteps, if you will. But the 99-Sense Theory (shortened to *99-Sensism*) obviously has been following him all along, even across continents, and disturbing not only his ideal life (marriage and family) but also the lives of those who appear to love and/or understand him. The funnily interesting (globalization) paradox in this whole mulovundism affair is that

---

[4] If sex is so primary to the definition of love, then would it not be hard to talk of a parent's love for his/her child, brother's love for his sister, etc. without involving incest? Incest is defined by the specialists as sexual intercourse between family members and close relatives. The term may apply to sexual activities between individuals of close "blood relationship", members of the same household, step relatives related by adoption or marriage, or members of the same clan or lineage. The incest taboo is and has been one of the most common of all cultural taboos: both in current nations and many past societies. Most modern societies have laws regarding incest or social restrictions on closely consanguineous marriages. In countries where it is illegal, consensual adult incest is seen by some as a victimless crime. See http://en.wikipedia.org/wiki/Incest; and Beaujot (1992: 290-91).

[5] http://en.wikipedia.org/wiki/Family. For further extensive discussion the concept of socialization, see Avison and Kunkel (1992), and for an elaborate take on the 'Definitions of Marriage and Family', see Beaujot (1992: 286-880.

Momany often suffers because of his 99-sensical appurtenance whereas he is or appears to be a 99-senser only in name or of a different and rare class that is here styled *globavillagism* – but not exactly what is being condemned by some experts as financialization.[6]

The 99-Sense Theory and Question

You can easily pick up his globavillagist or 'all-encompassing' stance from Momany's reaction to the following 99-sensical question, posed to him by someone in Montréal (Canada). "Why do you not attend Bangwa meetings?" Momany took a close look at his questioner and asked back: "Does that diminish the fact that I am a Bangwa-99-Senser?" Like most ethnic groups in Cameroon,[7] the Bangwa's epithet is 99-Sense; with some explanatory attachment that they are so craftily clever that they would not sell you a hen (but only a cock) for fear that it would produce chicken for you, thus preventing your coming back to buy from them. I do not know how far or correct this epithetical thesis (as all the others) could expound the attitude of most of the Bangwa people (including Momany and his family members, of course) that you will be meeting in this book as elsewhere (such as in Fossungu, 2013a). You will be the judge; but Momany was not yet done with his nose-poking questioner. "By the way," he further cross-examined his interrogator, "what am I to benefit from always flocking around with people who have ninety-

---

[6] Citing Foster and Magdoff' s celebrated 2009 book on the causes and consequences of 'The Great Financial Crisis', Weis and Fine (2013: 228) define financialization as a situation where "the traditional role of finance as a helpful servant of production has been stood on its head, with finance now dominating over production." For further excellent discussions of the issues of financial globalization and paradoxes, see Ferguson (2008); and Rodrik (2010).

[7] To give you some few examples, the Bameleke's is *Famla* – a sort of witch-crafting way of making wealth or what Fossungu (2013a: 29) would be describing as *"nyongo* (a money-giving, human-eating cult)"; the Béti's is *Chop Broke Potism* or people who do not think of tomorrow with money (see Panky, 1997); for Banyangi's females, it is *Ashawo* or prostitutes; for people from the North-West Region generally, it is *Come No Go* (see Orock, 2005); etc.

nine [per cent] senses like me?" His questioner was obviously stunned and perplexed; so Momany helped him out by indicating that he thought he could be a better Bangwa by not narrowing himself to Bangwa but rather associating with all in a bigger picture setting (like Cameroon Goodwill Association of Montreal – CGAM) because "in that way I can easily pick up that one percent sense that the Bangwa is missing and become a 100% human being while also sharing the ninety-nine percent I have with the 1% people. Just imagine a world with a lot of 100% or near 100% human beings!" Yes, indeed; this gentleman clearly views the world globavillagistically.

Unlike the Greek Cypriots with their Den Xehno,[8] Momany also greatly likes to *lovundelear* (love, understand, and learn from) the opposite sex. But how is he to find such love, understanding, and learning with his household's farming religion and both arms of the 99-Sense Theory always stubbornly standing in the way? As you will discover in this book, 99-Sensism does not only have two arms or sides (inside and outside) but also many 'inside' variations. Briefly put here, the outside arm refers to the perception of the 99-sensers by the non-99-sensers while the inside arm squarely deals with the actual comportment of the 99-sensers themselves that leads the others to often fear having serious dealings (like marriage and family) with them. No one doubts "that the study of families is an important avenue for the study of society" (Beaujot, 1992: 283).Knowing all that, the next issue requiring "levelling out [that] could be vital to understanding and appreciating this study" (Fossungu, 2013b: xiii) becomes that of what makes Momany's narrative on love and understanding important?

---

[8] As Zembylos (2013 : 19) tersely notes, recent ethnographic research shows that the teaching of *Den Xehno* (or "I'll Never Forget") in Greek-Cypriot schools essentially transmits the grand narratives of the Greek Cypriot community about the Turkish invasion of 1974, while it ignores the perspectives of the Turkisk Cypriot community or fails to make a distinction between Turks and Turkish Cypriots.

Why Is the Story of Momany Important?

The epicentre of this book, Momany is a young man full of diverse talents; and Fossungu (2013a: 2-18) narrates lengthily that he was born in a Bangwa village but raised in the city by an uncle that adopted him after his biological father died when the boy was just about six. Momany is there shown to have a lot of siblings both in and out of the household he grew up in but the following in the household will feature most prominently in this book: among the many sisters are Beatrice and Josephine; while from the lot of brothers are Vincent and Joseph. There is, of course, his father or papa and mother or Mami Thecla; and (out of the household) his birth mother or Mami Regina. As Momany has clearly underlined, he is not sharing his story to get pity from anyone (*id*: 58); and I truly think he clearly does not need that. In his proper words to this author,

I am doing so solely because a lot can be learnt from it by a lot of people, whether or not they are facing similar [exclusionist] situations. Those facing situations can also get inspiration while those not, will better appreciate the fact that they are not. I am not at all bitter and never would be toward any of the 99-sense theory adherents [from both inside and outside]; because if I never was bitter growing up in the household for all those many years, I am yet to find that thing that will make me bitter. Of course, people have this penchant for mistaking my bitter truth for bitterness in me; which is normal in the sense that a lot of people are not raised like me to have 'four eyes' by which to easily see the difference.

Four-Eyesism: Farsightedness or Africanscience?

Most Africans believe in witchcraft and/or sorcery (which I have more elegantly styled africanscience in this book) to the extent that even very rudimentary things like farsightedness are attributed to it. One of the popular ways to describe someone that is able to visualize what they often fail to see is to say that the person in question "has four eyes" – which leads one to wonder whether or not they are including the two normal eyes and the other extra two from africanscience? I pose this query because every scientist, Reaves (1992:20-24) theorizes, is interested in finding out about something, understanding it. Whatever a scientist wants to find out about, there are four basic goals that can contribute to that understanding; namely, (1) description, (2) prediction, (3) explanation, and (4) control. Does four-eyesism or africanscience also involve all of these basic goals? And which branch of four-eyesism, by the way? As will be seen, four-eyesism also has two arms or connotations (farsightedness and witchcraft) in this book and there is much talk of the apparent influences of both arms in this narrative on love and understanding. Better watch out then!

Quite apart from its additional 'four-eyesismatic' praiseworthiness, Momany's story is not just significant to only those facing or not facing situations (as he has particularly intimated). It is also most importantly worthy because his philosophy of (or approach to) love and understanding not only deals with love from a much broader and interdisciplinary angle than just the love-making (or having sex and associated pleasures) that most love stories seem to solely focus on. It also crucially raises and brings some new and sometimes wholly revolutionary or ground-breaking perspectives (and terminologies) on the subject-matters of love and understanding, of marriage, and of family. Of course, categories of research are seldom exclusive and individual studies often fit into more than one category (Reaves, 1992: 11). This one is no exception but is basically descriptive and exploratory, yet it will surely leave many experts (already warring heatedly on practice and theory, as seen in the opening of this introduction[9]) with a lot more to ponder

---

[9] Also, the constant 'supremacy' fights between theorists of the academia and practitioners in the professions/fields have led one startled academician to interestingly question: "Is university research not practical? If we look at the purpose of academic research, we have to include fairly high on the list the need to get published to gain access to the community of researchers, to pass its rites of initiation, to get tenure. Surely that is a practical purpose, and reading some of what gets produced along the way to promotion and tenure convinces me that this rite of

about and do further theoretical and applied or evaluation research on.

Telling Momany's love-and-understanding story is important, in addition, because a child rightly deserves to know if, when and why he or she is growing up in a broken home and parents and other relations that conspire not to tell this child the truth (at some point) do not deserve to be parents to that child in the first place (Fossungu, 2013a: 102). This precise and indispensable child-right to knowledge extends as well to those many children whose own ideal marriages/families never materialized or worked solely because of the self-serving machination of the parent(s) or what the dictionary of this book describes and condemns as *scholaparentism*; a deplorable comportment that has particularly affected the lives of some many children and would-be spouses, not only that of not only the village-city multidimensional man.

The Village-City Multidimensional Man

Momany has a lot of names (some of which you will come across) that are all tied to his adroitness (or lack thereof) in certain fields. I do not quite know if Momany is also one of such names or why this is his dominant name in this book but I suspect his parents or name-givers must be cutting something short in the name. The important thing right now is that this lad grew up not getting or enjoying the normal family love that often comes naturally with growing up in the bosom of one's biological parents (mother especially) and he seemed to have shrewdly found and developed *spelovundism* (some special kind of love and understanding) with some females outside the household, the inhibition of the household's farming religion notwithstanding.[10] The question remains though as to whether Momany did not open his 'four eyes' wide enough to

---

passage is often of more concern than developing and communicating a deep understanding of any particular phenomenon" (Watkins, 2001, 382).

[10] This religion has not just been inhibiting Momany love-wise but it has also been sagaciously converted by him into a very useful tool for "Surviving ... Across Continents" (Fossungu, 2013a: 19-47).

appreciate just how much love (and understanding?) was/were actually within the household for him. Well, let me not be the one to quickly spoil your story: just read on and discover for yourself how mulovundism (mutual love and understanding) or the lack of it/them can be palpable ingredients of success and/or failure in life.

Momany is not only an inter-continental, international, and multidimensional man; he is also a man with multiple relationships and who has lived and still dwells in a multitude of cities, holding a host of academic certificates and practising a chain of professions, including teaching and farming. I can begin to see some people wondering just how a reader without a penchant for multidimensionalism and other multi-isms would be able to grapple with Momany's somewhat unique 'philosophy of love and understanding'. I was myself thrown off on first encounter with his interestingly intricate and eye-opening story; not to even mention the vast array of its love and understanding terminologies like the few you have encountered this far. I can, nevertheless, assure my readers, first, that the terms are not very problematic grasping, new to you as they may be. Secondly, that I have done my best to scale down this complexly diverse character to easily digestible components; doing so without, on the other hand, inflicting much injustice or damage to his successes and failures in the domains of love and understanding (and, therefore, also of marriage and family), of 99-Sensism, and of his multifaceted goals that are captured in the predominant objective of the "bringing [of] more happiness to the greatest number of persons possible" (Fossungu, 2013a: ix).

Some sure ways of reducing the burdens of Momany's multifariousness, for instance, are to limit the cities of his residence here to just those that have impacted heavily on the issues of discussion; as well as using some enlightening conversations. Said cities are curiously concentrated in three provinces (out of ten) of each of the two dominant countries – Cameroon and Canada. For Cameroon, three of them are in the South West Region: Victoria (also known as Limbe), Kumba, and Muyuka (and precisely in its suburbs of Yoke and of Mpundu); two in the Littoral Region: Manjo and Douala; and one in the Centre Region: Yaoundé, the capital of the country. In Canada, there is Edmonton in Alberta, London in Ontario, and Montréal in Québec. The enlightening and entertaining use of direct powerful dialogues (between Momany and his numerous friends or other acquaintances) would also be a helpful way out of the complexity; and would already involve the 99-sensical one above as well as the one with Solomon that opens the first chapter.

The Chapters in Brief

As already noted, 99-Sensism has many inside versions, including an edition that is implicit in the household's farming religion as can be amply seen in the first chapter that deals with Loving, Understanding, Teaching and Learning from Women, with special focus on the first four women loved by Momany: since these women all seem to have helped enormously in constituting the bed-rock of the man's near inimitable philosophy of love and understanding. Chapter 2 begins the study of Momany's spousal quest, demonstrating and wondering if the expedition has been so blessed with a lot of Love and Understanding but 99-Sensism would have been responsible for transforming the Spouse-to-be into a Spouse-never-to-be. This Chapter largely focuses on and examines the woman that Momany first lost as wife while the next chapter hinges on and studies the one that he eventually married; both chapters seeking always to comprehend the love and understanding qualities of both women (as well as the host of others between/after them) as ideal spouse for the man with the vision which Momany has. This chapter-arrangement could be justified in the sense that the Yoke Conspiracy leading to the loss of Anna (in chapter 2) appears to have had slowing-down effects on Momany's objectives very similar to those of the re-conceptualization of family and marriage in Canada by Schola who Momany had thought was a real blessing from both the Yoke Plot and the other "Yaoundé... far-reaching and near-inexplicable spouse-quest gaffes" (Fossungu, 2013a: 119). Chapter 3 thus critically examines that new meaning of family in Canada in the context of beliefs in africanscience or witchcraft, while chapter 4 deals with some of the said spouse quest gaffes that obviously led Momany to Schola – still putting the accent on the seasoned avoidance of always tending to rush to explain any apparently inexplicable incident or occurrence with africanscience. The book generally shows how some parents (with questionable love and understanding for them) can be unashamedly ruinous to their children and children's children simply to attain their (parents') own egoistic ends, a tendency described in it as scholaparentism; an enterprise which, by the way, is neatly facilitated most of the time by Momany's own obvious failure to stick to some clear and dear principles handed down to him by his first, effective, and understanding lover, who also dominates the book's conclusion.

Chapter 1

Loving, Understanding, Teaching, and Learning from Women: The First Four Women and the Farming Creed

Learning then also appears to be opportunistic for men like Kamran and Muzaffar, who have been at the bottom of the social hierarchy. It is represented by the ability to grab opportunities that may come their way, sometimes quite unexpectedly, and the willingness to explore new sources of knowledge and experience [Rao and Hossain, 2012: 426].

Conversationally Getting into a Big-Hearted Man's Mind and Ways

Momany seems to decidedly have a destiny with *many* as this impressive conversation between his bosom friend and himself (at the University of Yaoundé – UNIYAO in the mid-90s) can show. Listening attentively to Momany talking about making tradition by breaking tradition (see Fossungu, 2013a: 49-50), Solomon stared at him for a while, admirably, before bursting out: "You see! I call you *Power* but I think your powers are so limitless and amoeba-like that you are always breaking virgin grounds, sometimes without even realizing it yourself." Momany asked Solomon what he was implying, wondering to himself whether Solomon was actually entailing his being a sort of the "virgins' man". "I simply mean that," Solomon elucidated, "maybe I should not just be calling you *Power* but must also describe you as 'a man of many rare talents'." Solomon was obviously making quite some sense but Momany kept wondering to himself if Solomon's virgin ground breaking theory could be behind his *virgiluckism* (being as lucky with virgins as he has been)? Did the virgins have a unique way of recognizing that he (Momany) was better at *virgibrookism* (the 'breaking' virgin grounds) or what?

1

"Power!" Solomon interrupted the virgin lingering;[1] asking to know what other virgin ground Momany was about to break. The latter simply insisted in response that Solomon too was just as powerful and must also be called *Power* in return. Solomon laughed and said it was not true. After Momany had lined up just a few of Solomon's own many academic and other achievements, Solomon suggested that he would be legislative while Momany be executive power.[2] Momany told him that was nonsense because power is power and if Solomon wanted to separate it the way he was going, who then was to be judicial power? At this point Solomon could not resist disclaiming the name completely and reverting to his virgibrookistic ('virgin ground breaking') postulation. He was only converted, baptized, and confirmed by Momany's sapient indication that if he would not be *Power* for any other reason, he has to be for the mere fact that he (Solomon) has also had to be a well known *girlimelighter* (a man in the glare of publicity for many women) but has no wife fiasco like Momany. Convinced as he was, Solomon insisted all the same that Momany was 'a man of many'.

Indeed, Solomon could be right about Momany and one of the most distinguished of his many professions, teaching, can now be taken to further demonstrate or corroborate. Several people who are lucky to become teachers usually exercise their calling in one institution and level but Momany has had no bounds in the levels and

---

[1] Virginity is defined by Wikipedia as the state of a person who has never engaged in sexual intercourse. There are cultural and religious traditions which place special value and significance on this state, especially in the case of unmarried females, associated with notions of personal purity, honor and worth. Like chastity, the concept of virginity has traditionally involved sexual abstinence before marriage, and then to engage in sexual acts only with the marriage partner. http://en.wikipedia.org/wiki/Virginity. See also S.C. Gallman's *Wise and Foolish Virgins: White Women at Work in the Feminized World of Primary School Teaching* (2012), as reviewed by Chikkatur (2013: 114); and Beaujot (1992: 300-303, 290).

[2] Solomon is, of course, implying here that Momany is still more powerful than he is; deriving, no doubt, from the perception of the almighty position of the executive branch in Cameroon particularly and (Francophone) Africa generally. For further exploration of the issue, see Fossungu (2013b); and Pratt (2007).

2

institutions he has had the opportunity to teach at, in Cameroon: Université de Yaoundé; University of Buea; Université de Douala; Institut d'Études Commerciales MATAMFEN, Yaoundé; Collège de l'Unité de Manjo; Unity Comprehensive College, Ekondo-Titi (South West Region); Progressive Institute of Stenography, Bamenda; Collège Protestant de Ndoungué (Littoral Region); Comprehensive College, Baba, in North West Region; etc. Momany does not only teach; he also learns in return, especially from women.

Women as First Teachers

When they think of women, a lot of men think only sex and associated pleasures. A woman, to Momany, is first and foremost a teacher. He is not by any means saying that men cannot teach men (of course, he learnt a lot from his father, grandpa, and many uncles, as shown by Fossungu (2013a)). In line with his reply to the 99-sense question, he is simply indicating that it is often difficult for "birds of the feather always flocking together" to learn any new skills. Now, also imagine (after completing this chapter) what Momany would be like today if it was not Miss Mandengue but a Mr. Mandengue that was his first school teacher, and you would have adequately grasped the gist of the Bangwa-99-Sense demonstration above in favour of men learning from women and vice versa. Maybe Momany is the odd man here, but he particularly enjoys a woman's company only when – in addition to what men usually want from them – he can get to learn from, and teach, them. Could this penchant in the man perhaps explain why there are very few women mentioned in this book that did not specially influenced him by aiding him in one way or other to realize or develop or confirm some uniqueness in himself and/or themselves; thus impacting on his life and philosophy of love and understanding? Could this idea also partly explain why Momany has had to date or lovundelear many women? Could it all be the result of his love having been awakened at such an early age? Perhaps he thinks this way because women happen to have been his very first teachers, informally and formally, beginning with his birth mother? How can Momany's somewhat 'strange' relationship with his first

3

school teacher (who was in principle not even the first) be explained? Can the *emeldalisation* of the love and farming prelude not be a better highway to some possible answers?

Emeldalising the Farming and Love Prelude

Momany is very proud of the man he is, including being Bangwa. But he is obviously not the type to be seen pigeon-holed into some limited and limiting categories. Of course, categories are contested and complicated in everyday lives, in social movements, and in classrooms, as Weis and Fine (2013: 226) lengthily explain. As critical ethnographers, they carry on, we therefore must seek to understand how individuals make sense of, resist, embrace, and embody social categories, as well as how they situate "others" in relation to themselves, often essentializing and reifying bordering "other" in their lives. This is precisely, they conclude, why our work as social analysts requires that we take a critical analytic stance on social arrangements and with respect to the narratives (and the quantitative patterns) we gather. I can, without fear of contradiction, tell Weis and Fine one thing here. That Solomon might not have gathered all of Hempel's "all the facts up to now" (cited in Sanders, 2010: 30) but he seems to have done his 'quantitative pattern' homework well when he uses the word "amoeba-like" to describe Momany. A whole volume of its own can be written on this man's perspectives but love and understanding are in the driver seat here.

Momany was in a single-sex boarding college which meant that he could most probably lovundelear (love, understand, and learn from) girls only out of school, during holidays. But the household's farming religion took every slim chance away from him to the point that Momany had to carry out a Market Day Revolution in order to get Wednesday, the Yoke market day, off the household's religion (see Fossungu, 2013a: 35-36). This audacious revolution on 'tradition' could no doubt be the handiwork of the spelovundism (special kind of love & understanding) already developed in the lad? He did advance certain reasons in his strong farm argument for having the Market Day off farming but these may not be the actual force

4

underlying that Revolution. The real reason behind the market day thing, I suspect, was not the one he stated in the farm argument. Rather, it would appear that Momany was looking for the opportunity to also meet girls like other 'college boys' "want[ing] to be respected" (Rao and Hossain, 2012: 426). Yoke being a farming community, it is on the market day that all the girls could be easily seen and if you were not around the market that made you a loser, to begin with. Momany seems never to have liked that position, especially not with the ladies (from whom he often lovundelears a lot); and holding testimony to it (as well as to love and understanding begetting success in life generally) is his fascinating market-day encounter with Emelda.

Based and schooling in Mamfe (South-West Region), Emelda is a glittering ebony black beauty that made lots of waves in St. Joseph's College, Sasse, Buea (where Momany was then schooling) with her stunning photos and juicy love letters. Yoke is such a small rural milieu in the not so big town of Muyuka and any outside beauty like Emelda would be very easily detected. Emelda was in Yoke for holidays at her grandpa's and seemed to have been on the verge of going back to Mamfe when it all happened, thanks to the Market Day Revolution. There she was that Wednesday morning, marvellously dressed and walking so confidently and fully aware of the vibes she was causing along the main Victoria-Kumba highway that crosses the locality; obviously heading towards the Yoke Market. She was still far from Momany's house that is not far from the market and he decided not to wait until she gets by the house, walking up towards her. It was a sort of drama for sure; but (from his unique primary school experiences to be discussed shortly) Momany was already used to it, as well as to intimidating-looking girls like Emelda.

As Momany approached, Emelda seemed to have correctly divined his intention and became even more hostile and prepared her 'keep-off' missiles. When he said "Good morning, my lovely Beauty," her rude reply was "There can be nothing good about the morning when a village boy like you keeps disturbing me in the hope of getting me to bed. Get out of my way!" He stood his grounds, telling

5

her politely that she was wrong on all fronts. That was a real tranquilizer, for she appeared then to look at him closely and asked what he meant. Momany then said, first, "I am not the type that capitulates at the first few shots; and, the rest I can only explain, if you really want to know, when we are comfortably seated and having a drink. Would you mind?" The hostility had by now gone and she smiled, saying: "By the way, I am Emelda." He said he was Momany but adding an effective hook that he was popularly known as Figaro in Sasse College. "You mean you are in Sasse? I am in Okoyong." He simply ushered her to the socializing spot around the market where they got to know more about themselves over a couple of drinks.

Emelda was a virgin at the time and she and Momany had so much in common: Both Bangwa, they were in single-sex colleges, having great ambitions; their fathers both worked with the electricity corporation, Sonel (société nationale d'électricité); their love for certain things was almost equal and endemic: always speaking in English (not Pidgin), dressing well, taking photos, listening to music, and writing letters to each other during school period. Because of Momany, Emelda became so attached to Yoke and farm work and thereafter never missed a holiday away from her grandpa, still coming to and living in Yoke even after his death. Because of Emelda, most of the girls in Yoke, and Muyuka generally, that might have been considering themselves as tough nuts to crack simply broke up for Momany because she loved walking around town with him, arms over shoulders, expressing her love in public without nervousness or fear – just like two of Momany's childhood lovers who so wonderfully shaped and directed particularly his love and academic life.

Emelda observably reminded Momany a lot about his first two real lovers – Annastasia and Rita – who also compare and contrast significantly with her (Emelda) but all three of them are heavily tied to the household's farming religion, an indispensable roadmap that has been charting, as well as obstructing, Momany's advance to university education and marriage; marriage being a type of union he sees as uniquely based on mutual love and understanding or

6

mulovundism. But Annastasia and Rita are not the first two women Momany ever fell in love with, being actually third and fourth. Their priceless roles in and influences on his life generally and his love and understanding narrative particularly may not be correctly figured out without the two women before them – MTU Girl and Miss Mandengue. Very briefly put, if MTU Girl awakened the love bug in Momany and Miss Mandengue the academic one, it is Annastasia that ingeniously nurtured and protected both bugs before Rita came along to creatively teach them how to stay apart even while working and walking together. It would thus be appropriate to examine the first two women he fell for together before the next two, without, of course, losing sight of the interconnectivity between and about them.

Miss Mandengue and Presbyterian School Yoke

Any talk about the time Momany spent in Presbyterian School Yoke would almost exclusively be one about Miss Mandengue. Momany cannot tell exactly when he left the place he was born in for the city of Victoria. He does not also know exactly for how long he had stayed with his new family before entering primary school; knowing only that the baby his mother was breastfeeding at the time of his arrival was born in 1966. From the fact that Momany never repeated a class and that he got to secondary school in 1975 and at the age of fifteen, Momany actually was eight when he began his primary school journey in Catholic School New Town, Victoria. It then quickly meandered around like some rivers and mysteriously ended there. That is certainly something special; but Victoria is not important only because of that. It is also the town his family has been most associated with; also being where his family was based during his secondary school, high school, and university years, and until his father's retirement and death. Miss Mandengue's defining role in Momany's life cannot be suitably grasped without (1) his first nickname in the household and (2) MTU Girl.

7

Momany's First Nickname in the Household

Momany's first nickname in the household is *Momany-Tekam-Uhm* (shortened here to MTU). When he had arrived Victoria Momany was speaking only the Bangwa language that was widely spoken then in the village; not understanding English or French, not even Pidgin or *Kamtok/Mbokotok* (see Ngefac, 2010). Bangwa that he could then speak was not spoken in the household and he was always chastised every time he spoke it (see Fossungu, 2013a: 36-39). Except for Josephine, everyone at home was always making fun of him by talking in Pidgin (and rarely in English) that he did not comprehend and the only thing he usually would say was *uhm*? (His way of saying "what do you mean"?) Hence, the slamming of the MTU nickname on him; a nickname that only Josephine in the household, it must be stressed, seemed not to be interested in pestering him with. This rare comportment quickly gained her Momany's quiet admiration, the more so as they were about the same age. Why was she the only one who understood his situation, he kept wondering to himself (but did not quite correctly employ the batteries of his clock-ticking head?).

Momany began school in Catholic School New Town where he attended for just two days before his father was transferred to Yoke. When they moved from Victoria to the Powercam camp in Yoke, Catholic School Muyuka had no available places in class one. So, while Josephine and Vincent attended it, Joseph and Momany got into Presbyterian School Yoke. You can see that his first two days in school were in Victoria but Momany cannot even remember who the teacher was, let alone the sex. Miss Mandengue (he also never got to know her first name) was therefore Momany's first school teacher. But that is not the only reason he remembers her so well. Always speaking only English, Miss Mandengue was like the much younger identical twin sister of Momany's biological mother. Momany never heard her talking in Pidgin in all the two or three years he spent in Presbyterian School Yoke. To him, this lady was so endearing and caring, dressing very cutely, and looking very learned and intelligent. I am not sure I know whether or not Miss Mandengue incarnates and confirms Gallman's "gendered images of 'good' and 'bad' teachers;

8

the gendered structure of labor and the economy; the role of 'love' in choosing teaching as a career path; and the expectations of 'niceness' and compliance from those who choose this career path" (Chakkatur, 2013: 104). What I understand though is that Miss Mandengue was the centre of attraction for all the male teachers of the school and certainly other 'strange' pupils like Momany. You will not want to believe that at his age then Momany fell so deeply in love with his first teacher. But that is exactly what it was. Much as he respected and adored her, Momany did not fear Miss Mandengue. Believe it or not, he even had the intention of telling her that he was that much in love with her as soon as he could communicate in English, a language that had supposedly brought about his first nickname in the household – "a nickname that taught me a lot about women, learning [much more quickly], and the difference between fear and respect" (Fossungu, 2013a: 36).

The first thing Momany then did (and it is not exactly clear to know how he did it) was to go to Miss Mandengue's table one day when most of the pupils were out playing during break. She asked what the matter was and, from the little English phrases he had already acquired from her teaching, he made her to understand (it is again miraculous that she did) that he was null in English and earnestly wanted to speak and write it just like her. Speaking here from my own experience as a long-time teacher, most teachers at this point would simply have sent the boy away with an empty and bland okay. Not Miss Mandengue who seems to have been destined to be the one to awaken the academic worm in Momany. She placed the little 'lover-boy' on her lap, very pleased that he even knew that he had a special difficulty, and gave him a small short lecture. Just sitting on her lap, Momany was feeling like he was already king of the world and sincerely wishing that her lecture never ended. That feeling and her instruction left an indelible mark in Momany's whole being; also effectively effacing the lingering MTU Girl love pains.

MTU Girl (and Mr. English and Mr. Big Heart)

She is simply known in this book as MTU Girl, for short, because there is another very important lady in Momany's life bearing the same first name as her and I do not want both confused when that name is used. MTU Girl, born to Nigerian parents in Cameroon, is the very first female ever to catch Momany's eye. In other terms, she whipped up the love thing in this little boy and at an age not normal for falling in love, assuming that he is a normal child. Very light-complexioned to the extent of being effortlessly confused for a métis, MTU Girl was living in the building next to Momany's in Church Street in Victoria. She was indeed a universally accepted beauty and the proof was in the number of guys that flocked in from far and near to seek her attention; a task made especially easy for them by the fact that her mother was operating a sort of street eating house. Several boys came there to eat but were actually there because of MTU Girl, since she aided her mother in the business. Because of the English language barrier, Momany developed a way of admiring her from a distance and, of course, she evidently knew he was dying for her.

Momany so much wished he was already speaking and understanding the English language. That is partly why his sister, Josephine (then in class three or two), often "caught" him looking at her books as if reading them. Josephine was surprised since she was quite aware that Momany could not possibly be reading or even understanding a thing in them. Being almost zero in Bangwa (but how could she even have taught Momany English in Bangwa?) and his English being non-existent, Josephine would often just stare at him, smiling very admirably; sometimes even trying to explain things in the books, as Momany imagined then. He already knew Josephine liked him very much and he liked her as well; but they became even more closely pulled together on this account and it is certain that Momany would have easily caught up with Josephine's "teaching" (whatever it was) if she persisted in doing it in *only* English. It is as if the door to Momany's brain had automatically closed itself off to any

10

new language that was not 'Good English'. Josephine thus became Momany's favourite sibling and some sort of very strong bond was developing between them, an attachment that was soon to be inexplicably loosened most probably by two things, viz., first, MTU Girl, followed by their father's job-related transfer to Yoke.

MTU Girl used to smile all the time with those guys eating there and it often hurt Momany until he realized that when she smiled his way it was a completely different beam. It was only then he appreciated that she just had to be nice to their customers; and that despite all the attention she was receiving from the others she liked him very much and wanted but him. Of course, saying he liked her too would be an understatement; but she obviously wanted him to be the one to break the ice or lead her on (to having her virginity to himself?). Doing that was not the problem because Momany badly wanted to do it and in such a perfect manner. He is a perfectionist in his way of doing things. But how could that happen when he could not articulate in the language she understood? Can only actions suffice in some of these things? Momany's dilemma got to a point he had to find out from Josephine (who had become so involved in trying to talk in Bangwa) how to briefly tell a girl something. His sister was so excited and asked what it was that he wanted to tell. Her excitement kind of surprised him a lot and he told her to forget it but she kept insisting on knowing but he never brought up the subject anymore.

Meanwhile it would seem like MTU Girl must have gotten so fed up with Momany's vacillation, or with what else, I do not quite know. As they passed by each other one day, the beaming did not come on as usual; instead it was his MTU nickname that he heard from her. It was a fatal blow because he was least expecting it. Momany did not mind that nickname at all from most of the folks. But when it came from this girl (the very first that he had fallen so much for, and quite knew also that she felt the same for him), it was a first love and psychological blow and he kind of lost his nerves for quite a long while. He asked himself many questions as to why she had not only suddenly ceased being nice but also called him the way everyone

11

(except her – until then – and his sister, Josephine) was doing? Why couldn't she just be like his sister Josephine, especially as he thought MTU Girl liked him very much? Every puzzle seemed to lead back to his hesitation in telling her how he felt about her and to lead her on. But could there be something else? Momany didn't quite know then but vowed to speedily learn to speak English so that he could confront this girl to know why she suddenly changed her attitude towards him. This could explain in part why his favourite sibling more often caught him looking at her books, the other part having to do with his intense desire to go to school.

Here then was Momany not only in school but actually feeling the person of another person he was feeling so much for – Miss Mandengue. He could then not remember ever sitting on the lap of a woman, let alone one as attractive and understanding as Miss Mandengue. He was wondering if her understanding was the result of her love for him; or, if (true) love cannot go without understanding, whether there could be understanding like Josephine's even where there is no love? His thoughts were cut short by the teacher telling him not to worry too much that he was void in English because all the other pupils were not better placed, emphasizing that she realised that he did not speak even Pidgin which, to her, was an immense advantage Momany had over the other pupils. She could possibly be right but Momany was so touched that he had tears flowing when Miss Mandengue set him down. (I do not know if the teacher intelligently knew the reason for her pupil's tears.) Miss Mandengue reassured the boy that everything would be fine, being very positive that he would excel in his studies. How come Momany could grasp all that this lady was saying and her understanding what he meant without a mastery of the language she was coming through? Could it have been love and understanding working through extrasensory perception? What was this unique feature on the left cheek that Momany shares with both her teacher and his birth mother?

That experience with Miss Mandengue was truly a defining moment for Momany; coming to permanently cement his being so special and destined for great accomplishments, a conclusion he had drawn from his having been "the one chosen out of so many disadvantageously placed [fatherless] village children whose chances of ever seeing a school classroom were very close to naught" (Fossungu, 2013a: ix). The journey from his village to *ncheng* (the coast in Bangwa) was indeed a whole mixed tale of its own (see Fossungu, *id*: 76-78) but the important thing is that it ended and Momany was then in Miss Mandengue's classroom initiating one of the longest short-cuts to university education and marriage/family. Because of *mandenguelovism* (his strange love for his first school teacher), Momany did not have any eye for any girl, in or out of school, for the whole year that he was in her class; nor involved himself in childish play with other children, not even often seeing himself as a child – quite apart from the definition of family in the household that somewhat excluded him from the child category. The days of the weekend simply became excessively longer and nightmarish than school days to Momany. He often spent his free time in school being tactically as close as possible to hear Miss Mandengue speaking English with others. Her voice had simply become music to him and he soon realized that the language was easier grasping than he had thought when it was her he was listening or talking to in class. Momany would have loved practising the language with her, one-on-one, at such free times but she was never left alone by the flocking attention seekers. He thus took to practising talking like her to himself at school and to "the pidgin speakers" at home and the camp. It was spectacular the way the magic of mandenguelovism – even as one-sided as it was – worked on him. He had become so proficient with the language by second term that he got the sobriquet of Mr. English at home; at the same time as having also established himself as Mr. First in Class, which he then undertook to keep on being.

Momany was by this time feeling really propped up and ready to beat the competitors over Miss Mandengue – *small pikin witi big big hart*, as most Pidgin speakers in Cameroon would be saying here. His plan of attack had been carefully designed. Finding another appropriate moment, Momany was to go up to Miss Mandengue and

13

ask if she could teach him something. If she said yes (as was surely to be the case), he was to say "Please, teach me how to love a woman as beautiful as you." It seems that his clock-ticking head had chosen this model for two reasons. First, he would have told Miss Mandengue right away what he wanted from her because he appeared to have learnt from the MTU Girl narrative that women generally do not like those who beat about the bush instead of going straight to the point. Secondly, this being a controversial topic (especially for a *small pikin*), it would readily provoke further discussion with her, during which conversation, Momany was confident, she would see just how different he was and thus fall in love with him, if she had not already fallen. That was what Momany had in store for the female teacher that meant so much to him.

The only thing that kept holding him back was this Mr. Okoro of a teacher; the only other Momany remembers from that school because he was the very impersonation of wickedness, having the official capacity of discipline master to vent out his evilness without remorse. Questioned by this writer if he was not confusing one thing for another, Momany instantly emphasized: "I surely know the difference between discipline and wickedness. I recall him well due to the manner he used to snake-beat pupils, for whatever reason. My later acquaintance in Sasse College on the Nigerian-Biafran civil war made me think this man perhaps had an issue to settle with Cameroonians for not having aided Biafra and was then taking it out on young school pupils." As he tersely added, his case with Miss Mandengue, if it got to them, would surely not have ended with just beastly trouncing (that he would have gladly taken because of his deeply-rooted love for her) but dismissal as well. Anything, anything whatsoever that even remotely had to affect his schooling in this way was to be shunned. He therefore put this beautiful miss aside after a year of balancing his acquisition of her love against the wrath of Mr. Okoro *et al.* According to Momany, it appears as if destiny was telling him not to play with the fire called Mr. Okoro but to instead concentrate on the girls where he lives. Momany reluctantly but determinedly took that wise counsel and turned to the Powercam

14

camp where Annastasia first gave him all the mutual love and understanding or mulovundism that he had until then not found, with Rita closely following up and perfecting it all in the Kumba school.

The Pivotal Roles of Annastasia and Rita

I will first talk about Annastasia and Momany's life in the Powercam camp before Rita and his life in the Kumba School, and then discuss some early applications of the influences of both ladies in the later stages of Momany's progress and/or retreat, which would flow into the subsequent chapters.

Annastasia and Momany's Life in Powercam Camp Yoke

There is not really much in actual love relationship to capitalize on regarding the two years plus Momany spent in the school in Yoke; with much in the domain instead being acquired from his living in the workers' camp. There were twelve numbered households in the Powercam camp in Yoke and Momany's family lived in Number Two, a joint building with Number Three. The entire building took the form of a capital E without the middle cut such that the kitchens of both households were directly facing each other. All the buildings in the camp were not identical, with only the one constituting household Numbers Ten and Eleven being identical to theirs. Two buildings in the middle of the camp had the complete capital E shape and each contained three households (Numbers Four to Six, and Seven to Nine). The remaining two L-shaped buildings consisted of single households (Numebers One and Twelve). The camp was well planned unlike those of other corporations like the Cameroon Development Corporation (CDC) as this was home also for many of the cadres of Powercam, with none of its workers being permitted to live out of the camp.

The camp was obviously bustling with life as every household had at least three school-going children, with the overall ratio of boys and girls being almost 50:50. Yet, the competition in the camp was as

15

if one sex far outweighed the other; a trend obviously tied to the fact that either a few girls had so many boys going after them or the other way round. Most of the girls were somehow more mature in both age and school standing than most of the boys. Having failed with MTU Girl in Victoria because of language barrier and with Miss Mandengue in the Yoke school because of the fear of dismissal, this camp is where Momany had his first practical lessons in the love and girls-winning domains, coming to the stance that he was a force to be reckoned with in the spheres. His constant worry however was that of treading carefully and without compromising his progress in school. Not that it was going to affect his performance in school, but that he was aware of what he was up against should there be any *faux pas*; especially so as one of his sister's Pepper Ordeal "certainly sent an always present cautionary message to my head as to the way I was to go about this boyfriend-girlfriend business" (Fossungu, 2013a: 41).

Having sort of boycotted or looked down on them for the past year and having also the Mr. English reputation, many of the girls in the camp were actually going crazy for him when Momany returned to the camp field. A *fisrtomulovist* (someone as yet to actually find mutual love) as he then was, Momany kind of liked them all because he did not then quite see any woman who, alone, could completely fill Miss Mandengue's gap in his 'big heart' and being. But one Ewondo or *chop-broke-potist* girl called Annastasia had the upper hand from both her standpoint and Momany's and she made very good use of the advantage. First, Annastasia approximated very much Momany's first teacher. She was not only very beautiful and about four or five years older than Momany but also the most senior of the girls (some of those in Momany's household apart). It also is very likely that she must have intimidated the others away from Momany. Furthermore, Annastasia was not only the first child (and only girl) in a family of four children, but also most significantly in household Number Three – nearness to raw materials, as economists and some geographers would say regarding the localisation of industries.

But there was a dangerously complicated catch to Annastasia. She was the most senior girl in the camp and one of Momany's senior

16

and bullying brothers, Vincent (also the most senior boy there and attending the same school in Muyuka with her), took it to be his natural right to have her; and Vincent did not hide this at all. So how was Momany to go about it? Surrender Annastasia to Vincent when she showed no interest in Vincent but in Momany? Was *Okoroism* (the Mr. Okoro syndrome) or *surrenderism* to be permitted to follow Momany all through his life? This was a decision of Momany's life. He weighed the competing options carefully and then unequivocally said "No More" to the surrendering trend and went straight for the girl. Annastasia also quickly *understood* the dilemma Momany was in and adjusted accordingly: should one not be inclined to smoothly theorize here that pure love always goes with understanding? Is it not the same thing Lionel Richie would be saying in his musical piece, *Love Will [Always] Find A Way*? The love pair therefore swiftly developed their unique way of communicating without raising the Vincent dust of suspicion – largely thanks to the nearness factor. For instance, Momany knew exactly what message Annastasia was sending by the position and posture she took in front of their kitchen or near the washroom door (which was not far from the kitchen); the same going the other way. It was working so well for them and they were having the best of times; having also surprisingly discovered they were each other's first. I am here sort of pondering on and leaving the experts to discover whether Momany's extreme virgiluckism or luck with virgins could be tied to the Annastasian DVB (double-virgin blessing). An important ingredient of success to Momany, Annastasia's (like Rita's) contribution cannot be tied down to any one place in this book but it could be sketched here through the two most pronounced arms of her love and understanding: (1) the automatic door and (2) *bolargumentalism*.

The Annastasian Automatic Door (AAD)

In a way, Annastasia made Momany to want to regret the year before he met her but he was still very glad because the Miss Mandengue year did not only help in academically defining him but also obliterated a possible repeat of the MTU Girl saga. It catapulted

17

him as well to the famous Mr. English that won him even the admiration of the parents of both the competing girls and his male rivals in the Yoke camp (see Fossungu, 2013a: 39-41). Everyone in the camp and beyond simply wanted to be around Momany to hear "Good English", as they often put it. Annastasia, his new found and first love ever, was particularly proud of him and although many women in her place would be very wary of this popularity, she was not. I guess the experts would agree with me for saying that this is exactly what love and understanding should entail. I also think she was mature enough to know herself well enough and, therefore, also the one she was dealing with – Momany. Momany also loved her so much and (in addition to/following mandenguelovism's cutting-off effect?) did not see the need for anyone else because he knew just how much love Annastasia also had for him. Annastasia was not only reciprocating his love for the first time in his life; she was also informally teaching him a lot. Momany quickly learnt from her that love and trust walk together and, as you will realize in due course, this has greatly defined his later relationships (positively and negatively). Love and understanding would appear to be all what Momany needs to bring out the best in himself, this also being seen in, and cemented by, an example of his lover-teacher's bold and strong arguments.

Eye-opening Bolargumentalism

Among other things, Annastasia made Momany discover the magic or strength of bold powerful arguments. This happened one day when the others had gone to farm and he was left home to babysit and cook, as usual. Someone had either betrayed them or Vincent was acting under mere suspicion when he came back home from the farm before the scheduled time and caught Annastasia and Momany "doing bad thing" or "doing papa and mama", as kids then variously referred to it. Vincent must "then have felt the same way a man would, knowing his wife has run off with another 'inferior' man" (Fossungu, 2013a: 157) and was simply about to eat Momany raw. But the lady stood very tall and defended her lover, telling Vincent that even if he should kill Momany she would rather die with

18

him than go out with Vincent; firmly concluding: "Just cause him any trouble and you will see what I will do to you." She then kissed Momany on the cheek and left.

Lovoldism is what Momany calls it; because this was the boldest thing (an act of love for that matter) he had until then witnessed from any woman. If sitting on Miss Mandengue's lap Momany had felt *like* king of the world, Annastasia's bold kiss in front of Vincent the hangman confirmed that he (Momany) was not just *Fonwancheng* (Vincent's birth father's kingdom³) but indeed and most crucially *Foncheng-allah* (king of *ncheng* and the entire planetary system). That is the flashback Momany had at that very moment because he had never before then seen the bully called Vincent looking so helpless in front of anyone except when he was being scolded by their papa and he had no defence. What is actually this power that women have over men that are so infatuated with them? Was Vincent really scared of Annastasia or just unbelievably wondering how 'Big-Head' Momany could have succeeded in doing with her what he himself had been unable to do? I do not know the alternative which is correct but I know that Momany's *vincentology* (the fear that Vincent was going to talk about catching them 'doing bad thing', to be followed by his own 'Pepper Ordeal') had vanished by the time Annastasia had left their house that day. And, frankly, it was no longer the Vincent-hide-hide between Annastasia and Momany and Vincent thereafter found it really hard to strike the small, big-headed boy the way he used to, not even when they got transferred to Kumba, far away from Annastasia.

As you can see, bold powerful arguments can, at appropriate moments, do a lot more than physical strength or force can. I do not exactly see how Annastasia could ever do anything physical to keep Vincent from doing what he intended doing to Momany but she had succeeded in keeping both vincentology and Vincent off her lover through her bold and strong argument. Momany not only learnt a lot from his papa on the score of not fearing him but also from the girl

---

³ Momany is, interestingly, also called Fonwancheng, being the namesake of Vincent's birth father.

that Vincent was trying to bully into his girlfriend. In other words, Annastasia was not only Momany's lover; she was indeed also his teacher-student; and a very effective one too. Like respect, love and understanding would obviously be a two-way street, if success (and not failure) has to be crowned. Momany also used Annastasia's bolargumentalistic strategy later, not against Vincent but using him, to win a physical battle that he would otherwise have lost in the school in Fiango, Kumba; a town wherein Rita carried him to another level of mulovundism *in* school.

Rita and Momany's Life in Sacred Heart School (SHS), Fiango, Kumba

Kumba occupies a very critically vital place in Momany's life. This is not only because most of his years of primary school were spent there but also because of the milestone accomplishments tied to it. By such deeds I am not just alluding to the Cameroon College of Arts and Sciences (CCAS) Kumba achievement – his obtaining the General Certificate of Education (G.C.E.) Advanced Level in Lower Sixth. It has to as well to some very important survival strategies he acquired there that have had to follow and guide him all along, both academically and otherwise. The mulovundism Momany acquired and enjoyed in SHS Fiango has played roles in the CCAS short-cutting process to university education that, without it, there might not even have been any road at all to cut, short or long. Indeed, while in Yoke Momany's non-academic success was out of school, in Kumba everything was concentrated almost entirely in school with Rita (a Bangwa) at the heart of it. This special lady's influence even in the later stages of his evolution is inestimable.

It was second term in class three when Momany arrived in SHS Fiango in 1971, being about two weeks later than the others in class. He was already used to being the centre of attention especially in the Yoke camp. But it was in this school that Momany really thought he was born to be at the centre of things, thanks a lot to Rita. As he was being introduced to the class, Momany swiftly noticed Rita. Not just because of her daunting beauty but especially because she was

20

sending away the other girl that was sharing the two-place bench with her. She very strategically had a place already reserved for Momany by the time the teacher asked him to find a place and settle down. How could he have rationally refused her appetizing and smiling invitation to sit by her? Just telling him her name alone (to leave out the sharp contrast in their complexion) had instantly flashed Momany's mind back to the woman with the same name who first awakened the sleeping love in him. Shining black in complexion, with very white teeth, Rita was one of the beautiful girls (if not actually the most attractive) in the school. Momany very intuitively knew at that moment that he was getting into something that invites lots of trouble. The tale of Annastasian lovoldism beating and suppressing vincentology was still there, fresh and burning, for Momany not to anticipate much trouble from being that 'new boy' associated with the gem called Rita.

Momany did not understand nor even heard a lot that was being taught that first day, often being lost most of the day in his own thoughts; or trying to let Rita know there was much time after the lesson to answer some of her stream of questions. His thoughts were still with Annastasia, for sure. How could it have been otherwise with his first love who also completely comprehended him that much? But these thoughts roamed on that day from one place to another to discover what was so special in him. If Momany had actually already written a test or exam in SHS Fiango, he would have been thinking that his performance was responsible. But here was he just arriving and this lovely girl (and evidently everyone's dream girl) was all over him, not having even shown restraint on her feelings towards him. What was it with him? If there was any small love-shyness still left in Momany, Rita obviously sent it evaporating as she took hold of his hand when the bell rang for break, saying "we are going to eat together." As they walked around towards the "dinning shed", Momany could see admiration in the eyes of some, much envy in those of many; and he murmured "Now go to work", obviously reminding his big clock-ticking head. When Rita asked what he had said, he responded: 'Good to walk [with you].' By the time the thirty-

21

minute break was over Momany was more popular in the school than most pupils who had been there for several years. But this kind of fame does not sit well with rivals and other detractors; and Momany surely had a lot of them.

Mbinchangalogist or Mr. Trouble

It was not long before a bigger boy, in Rita's presence, threatened to beat him up and get her. Instinctively recalling Annastasia, Momany did not show any sign of fright and boastfully told him to get a partner before the fight. But the bully was not affected and madly asked why Momany thought he needed to do that. As virgiluckism would have itself been blessed by the Annastasian DVB (double-virgin blessing), at that very moment Vincent was passing by, some distance away. Momany therefore unhesitatingly responded: "Because I will damage you completely; you see that big guy over there [pointing at Vincent]? I once crushingly beat him over a girl. If you like ask him for confirmation." Empty heads that most bullies are, according to Sam's Mother, he unthinkingly called Vincent's attention. Vincent who was a little bigger than him approached and the verification was positive since both bullies were individually thinking of two different kinds of beating – just like had Sam and his Mother (see Fossungu, 2013a: 39-40). The guy left immediately. Vincent also walked away like a real *ngong* (frightened and useless) dog with its tail between its hind legs.

It was a lot easier than Momany had expected. He was then thinking quietly, not about africanscience methods that some there present would be saying he might obviously have used in beating up the big Vincent bully, but instead about the name an aunty had given him. Mbinchang, his aunty who babysat him had explained to him (in Yoke where she continued using the name even as everyone was then calling him Mr. English), literally means Mr. Trouble (in Bangwa). So I am a troublesome child so to speak? Momany had asked. Not at all, she had answered. Then why give me such a name, he wanted to know. When you were a baby, you used to appear like someone who likes causing trouble; but it was my mistake, she explained. I don't still get it Aunty, he told her. "You see I was perfectly right. You have not changed and I knew then that it was just your nature. I gave you that name because you were different from all the other babies I had until then babysat." She was obviously taking her time and either raising his anxiety or just enjoying the baby she nurtured and could predict. Could you please explain the difference, aunty, he inquired. Unlike the others, she went on, "you were never following my instructions (e.g. sit there) without wanting to know why or how, or why not here, etc. This made me to learn a lot since I always had to find a justification for everything I wanted you to do." That is surely a lot of trouble for anyone that does not quickly get used to your comportment, his aunty added, before concluding that "I confirmed the name when I started seeing the way you dealt with other children who came around with any trouble."

If I understand Momany's aunty as I think I do, then *Mbinchang* is not the literal Mr. Trouble but Master of the Art of Trouble; just as Mr. English (*Mbi-Aleghe* in Bangwa) describes Momany's mastery of the English language, not that he is English language itself. Momany's quiet reflection had led him as well to pondering on how Vincent would want to deal with him at home for the ridicule; but the bully never even mentioned the matter. It seems that the Annastasian 'Doing Bad Thing' Lovoldism in Yoke completely paralyzed him in Momany's regard. What a precious gift from his first love! Momany was only awakened from his sweet thoughts by Rita who could hardly believe (like most of the others present there) that he had beaten someone as big as Vincent *over which girl?* Was this not more trouble for avoiding less trouble? He merely told her that his strength is in his head and not in his muscles, pointedly asking: "Have I not just beaten the bully that was threatening me over you?" Rita beamed so profusely and said "I see what you mean." Master of the Art of Trouble was surely working wonderfully, wasn't he? There could be no doubt that this Bully Incident, graced by mbinchangalogy, enormously contributed the unrelenting glue to the Rita-Momany mulovundism and thus resulted in the significant Ritaian Crisebacology.

The Ritaian Crisebacology

Crisebacology is the rare science or skill of Critical Separation-Balance/Cooperation of matters of the heart and academics; a capacity whose development is heavily tied to the Rita-Momany exceptional mulovundism. Let us see how it built up. Rita and Momany had simply become inseparable in school, sharing the same bench, class after class; her bold ways of often sitting so tight to him initially seeming to be some sort of new distraction. As you well know, Miss Mandengue had completely absorbed Momany during the one year he was in her class in Yoke; but it was more on the learning side and (apart from the short academic bug-awakening lap-lecture) Momany never ventured this close to her *in* or out of class, especially as there was the additional hindrance of her not even knowing how he felt about her. (Or, could she have intelligently known, having fallen for him also at first sight, but was just 'situationally' exercising restraint?) Annastasia too was not in the same school, let alone class, with Momany; theirs being a home thing. This one in SHS Fiango was then utterly new to him. Rita's *massa* or husband then became his other name; and not even being in her mother's classroom (in class four) provided any deterrence to Rita's amorous comportment in class and school. Like Annastasia, lovoldism was Rita's watchword, not *janodilism* nor *annaspectism* (both terms being different forms of one-way parent or sibling respect).

Momany had quickly understood from day one that Rita, contrary to the general trend then, was not a "spoiled child" but someone who, unlike most of them in the school and environment, had the rare opportunity of being brought up in a home where fear for parents and elder siblings/acquaintances was not the rule. In short, that she was not suffering from *janodilism* which this book (as chapter 2 lengthily shows) defines as the almost religious or unthinking fear of parents, elder siblings, and other senior school acquaintances that uncomfortably would be passing for, or hiding behind, 'respect'. The quick discovery further endeared Rita to Momany and he had to necessarily find a unique way to accommodate both her bold

24

companionship and his schooling. This was certainly the type of person that could easily see eye-to-eye with him on a lot of issues because of their reciprocal love and understanding – just like with Annastasia, who could have been the only one, perhaps, to effectively destroy what she had herself started: Momany's having just one lover, despite all the clamouring for him (the AAD effect). But that difficulty was swept away because Annastasia's father had also been miraculously transferred from Yoke to Yaoundé, as Momany 'mixed-feelingly' found out during the very first holiday from SHS Fiango.

In the household Momany had quickly learnt that most people (like his father) are not hostile against you as such but against some comportment or trait that you may be exhibiting. That once you can realize this and do your best to take away that trait or behaviour, the hostility goes with it. The fear that is consequent on the hostility also vanishes and both of you start relating in a very productive and mutually beneficial way (Fossungu, 2013a: 42). You have also amply seen this thesis holding good in Momany's absorbing encounter with Emelda in the Love and Farming Prologue above. So, why shouldn't Momany be able (unlike the others without 'four eyes') to see Rita for who she really is? And why wouldn't that knowledge make her more special to someone like him with this farming-religion handicap? Remember that farming was not only a holiday thing, being also an entrenched after-school activity in their household. Remember also that the Market Day Revolution took place when Momany was in college and in small town Yoke but this is primary school and in big town Kumba. Remember as well the importance of the "nearness" factor for Annastasia that even led to the 'doing of papa and mama'. This was clearly absent in Kumba with Rita.

Momany was truly fascinated by Rita's beauty and bold ways on the first day but it is her special character that really plunged him so deep into loving her and sustaining same. Needless to say it was equally reciprocal. It seems that Momany's clock-ticking head usually comprehends simple instructions (such as the murmured 'Now go to work') complexly. His head seemed to have correctly analyzed the complete situation and long-term consequences and, above all, created a separating/balancing-cooperating capacity between matters of the heart and academics (crisebacology); a facility that would prove very elastic and critically useful for the future. Momany had thus swiftly become conscious that Rita could not be allowed to be in complete control of the situation; that he necessarily had to be in the driver seat even as she gets her way. But he needed to convince her, not impose upon her; and how was he to do so?

He again drew heavily from the Annastasian bolargumentalism or wisdom of bold arguments doing a lot more than naked force. The SHS case is analogous to the invisible hand of 'true' federalism (see Fossungu, 2013b: chapter 2). This situation can also be likened to the stability/change developments that took place in the Ottoman Turkish polity which, according to political scientists, were of a completely different nature, leading Collin Hay to argue that not everything is 'resolved by an understanding that politics unfolds as a result of the interaction between actors and structures' (cited in Pratt, 2007: 195). Thus, the perplexing Ottoman Empire becomes what Göymen (2007: 220) calls "an excellent example of a state that first undertook reforms in order to reverse an unfavourable balance of power" through selective borrowing of "Western techniques and institutions in order to withstand Western assault and preserve the empire." The SHS-Fiango Continent was indeed a sort of Love Empire, I can then say. Momany had many rivals for Rita but she also knew well enough that she was not without rivals for him, one in their class that she particularly watched being Pamela – a very intelligent and pretty quiet Bamileke girl. Normally, if he had had enough time to look around before Rita got him hooked, Pamela would have been the one Momany would have liked to settle for, especially in order to stay away from the limelight in SHS Fiango (and would his life have been the same today?). But Pamela is not what Momany employed in reasoning with Rita. He rather opened up to her in a way about his life at home and in a way also killing the lingering Pamela suspicion. Efficiently killing two birds with one stone, most people would say; but I would rather talk about it in terms of love and understanding adorning success.

26

It was thus during third term in class three that Momany told Rita that the only reason he excels in school is that he has a magnetic brain; which somehow makes up for the fact that he does not have any time at all to study after school. "So my dear Rita, if I don't get it in class when the teacher is explaining it, I will never get it." She was apparently confused and must have been wondering ('Has this Pamela girl finally succeeded in taking him away from me?') when Momany clarified: "I am not saying that I don't want you near me in class. On the contrary, I have grown so used to having you do all what you do to me in class that I instead do not understand a thing the day you are absent and not by me in class. I am just trying to tell you, my dear Rita, why I have not been able to be with you out of school hours despite your numerous requests." Farm and house work so neatly combined to put out any other after-school activity for Momany. Rita stared at him while he was detailing the explanation and he found her even more beautiful than before. She brightened up copiously and hugged him, saying: "Momany, I now understand you more and the more I do the more I like the fact that I loved you on the first day my eyes fell on you. Thank you for your openness."

If Annastasia is credited with inventing it, then Rita would be responsible for perfecting it. I am talking about this automatic door that shuts everyone else out as soon as Momany finds bold and truthful reciprocal love. Love and understanding are keys to any successful relationship. I have wondered a lot about what the experts would say must have happened to Momany from classes three to six with Rita, if he had not been that open and decisive at the start? Would it be love and understanding driving him here? Was it the wise thing to do, especially for someone with objectives like Momany's (making life more worthwhile for the greatest number of persons possible)? Otherwise, would it not have been total disaster: viewing what formidable forces he was battling with within the household in order to attain those goals, and a lot of his energy being torn off by further love battles and uncertainties? Could this also begin to explain the development of the AAD and his entire love and understanding outlook?

Momany knew well enough that Rita also wanted him to be her first and there were several times he understood she badly wanted it to happen but they never 'did bad thing'; not because he did not want to. What he has so stridently emphasized is that what he has had with Rita no amount of sex could ever replace or take away. But I would venture to guess again that some mainstream love and sex experts would see him as selfish in regard of this woman (like Ray Parker, Jr., sings in 'A Woman Needs Love Just Like You Do').This issue was brought to the attention of Momany who responded as follows. "If bending its back to weather adverse conditions so as to preserve itself for the good of greater humanity makes the shrimp selfish, I would rather not be selfless. Imagine all the others I have had to aid in one way or other since completing primary school; and then imagine my schooling ending in SHS Fiango before class seven!" Listening to him, I could only say Wow! What a man! Whatever the sex-inclined love experts think, the important thing though is that Rita (like Annastasia) not only loved but also understood Momany and their relationship in school only grew from strength to strength over the years (true love is not just about sexual intercourse, some would say?), their hope being to go to the same boarding college one day and be together forever.

But Momany had just completed class six in SHS when his papa was transferred back to Victoria. These transfers and Momany's love life! Always together in class for three years, Rita and Momany were to be torn apart (just like had happened earlier with Annastasia) and it was no secret that they both ached and cried a lot. It was an emotional moment as he said bye to his second and in-school love in these lines: "I am just hoping that you will always understand that I am forever indebted to your love and understanding that opened my head to so many good things that have been so precious and handy during my stay in SHS and would certainly still be in my post-SHS life." Momany is, of course, referring particularly to the Ritaian crisebacology of not only love and academics, but other attributes that obviously enhanced both his *staying* powers in the household and his ability to *progress* in it; as could be seen in the reminder of his primary school evolution, and beyond.

Some Applications of the Annastasian and Ritaian Influences

The discussion in this section is in two segments, namely, (1) Charalicing from the Genesis of Momany's primary education to Sasse College, and (2) Susaglamouring in WWMSS-Mpundu, including Joan and studies at the UNIYAO.

Charalicing from Genesis to Sasse College

It is evident in the discussion; but those who specifically want to define it first could say *charalicism* is the art of venturing with irresistible risk, danger that directly leads you to surprisingly taste your first failure or first success (as the case may be) in any domain. How exactly then did Momany charalice from genesis to Sasse College? Returning to the genesis of his schooling in Victoria to complete class seven, Momany unfortunately did not find MTU Girl at the time that he was Mr. English and comfortably ready to confront her. I guess she must have left for further studies elsewhere, preferably in Nigeria. This time around, Momany's family was no longer renting but living in the family's own house in Mile One (directly opposite the Victoria General Hospital). Still suffering enormously from the brutal separation from Rita (the only love of his life for the three years in Kumba), he thought he needed a substantial break from the spotlight. It appears as if the AAD (Annastasian Automatic Door) was a necessary gift from nature since spotlight had to become his first name. As usual, most of the girls in his class and school were wild to have Momany but he made all their attempts fruitless since, first, he was not sure any of them could measure up to Rita; and, second, the AAD still had to operate by itself – the second A's job.

Nevertheless, with time, this Rita-like complexioned, Pamela-like quiet and beautiful Banyangi girl in his class kind of caught his eyes by second term. Bent on avoiding the spotlight (perhaps this evasion

29

was never meant for him), Momany had tried, to no avail – due to after-school farming – to meet this girl out of class or school. So he wrote Alice a note expressing how he felt about her and how he would like them to be lovers. Instead of privately replying to him, positively or negatively, Alice (for her own reasons) made it a public display, with anyone in school who wanted to, reading his high-powered love note to her. It was kind of very embarrassing for a guy whose attention many of the girls in school were actually seeking and not getting. Maybe, for acquiring mulovundism, Momany was never meant to go first after them but them after him first? With Alice he had his first real taste of failure and ridicule in the domain and he thereafter closed the damned door completely and concentrated solely on passing out of primary school in high-flying colours.

But that school-decision would seem to be questioned in Mile One where they were living by an Annastasia-like Bakossi girl called Charlotte. I call her Annastasia-like in the sense that (1) some love mishap in school led Momany to both of them; (2) both are his first in their various unique ways; (3) both have almost similar and very attention-grabbing wowing strategies; and (4) there is the Miss Mandengue role/effect with both. Charlotte was evidently everyman's dream girl; having this tantalizing pointing breastwork (*lolo*, as Ivoirians call it) and an appetizing backside (*makandi*, to Cameroonians). I am yet to find anyone that could then resist Charlotte; since she also knew how to wind her *makandi* so well that when she passed by most of the men had standing 'workmen'. Yes, indeed, she was so enticing but Momany had already shut the door here, just like he did to the Yoke camp because of Miss Mandengue (and to Church Street in Victoria because of MTU Girl?).

I do not know what had actually happened at their home that day but Charlotte was crying so loud and for so long that almost everyone in the quarter went by their house to find out what was amiss. She would still not stop the crying or let anyone try to comfort her. But as soon as Momany was approaching, she stopped crying and began giggling and smiling broadly. He then turned around to go and she went back to the old job, even louder. Momany got the message well enough and thereafter comforted her. Minutes later you could not believe she was the one that had been crying that much and for that long. It was a miracle to a lot of people. Her strategy for telling Momany it was him she wanted led to his being nicknamed "Charlotte's *Massa*" by Mile One boys and girls. Charlotte took it more seriously than Momany had thought and was actually going to start having children with him, as he realized. That was simply not good at all for his going to college (or university) and he quickly dropped out of the love-game before it could be too late. Charlotte's irresistibility was obvious but, to Momany, she became even more appealing after a good taste of her superb bed performance, coupled with her readiness to be available any time, and there was more. Yet, Momany was able to resist her when it had to do with disturbing his studies in any way. I guess if he could have stayed away from his birth-mother-like Miss Mandengue because of it, he surely would be able to do same to any other woman.

The issue though is that, as between Annastasia and Charlotte, I do not know who the experts would say actually took away Momany's 'virginity'. All I know is that he had something special with each of them that no other person, until each of them, had given him. I theorize as such because I fondly remember Momany talking about Stella, a Victoria virgin he had met after Charlotte, demanding that he should get up because he had 'urinated' in her and how his mind immediately flashed back to Charlotte with whom he first had that "urinating" sensation. Having this "urinating" consciousness was such a feeling with Charlotte, according to Momany, that maybe "I would have taken the high risk with Rita in Kumba, if I had already had this sensation with Annastasia in Yoke?" I could not help him with his query but the experts are here and perhaps could; meanwhile, it interesting that both Charlotte and Annastasia were out-of-school loves.

Back to the school arena and looking back, I am inclined to think Alice's comportment was a blessing in disguise to Momany – would she have synchronized with him like Rita at that critical passing-to-college year? Also as a blessing was his not being admitted to a government lycée, a failure which led him to Sasse College. Sasse being a single-sex or male-only college, had two noticeable effects on Momany. First, he felt the great and urgent need for the 'revolution' in Yoke that helped in bringing in lovoldious (bold-in-love) Emelda. Secondly, he did not feel the need to employ the most pronounced aspect of the Ritaian crisebacology until four years later when his "destiny with *many* refused to be put aside for secondary schools" (Fossungu, 2013a: 55). That is, when there were some petty differences between his class and the then high-handed school administration that saw only the dismissal of the entire class as the solution. A sizeable number of Momany's classmates (including him) ended up in WWMSS in Mpundu for the completion of the 1979/80 school year.

Susaglamouring in WWMSS-Mpundu: Africanscience Aiding?

WWMSS is the acronym for World Wide Missions Secondary School. Just having some connections with Sasse College is known to be enough to win over most girls. Imagine then a contingent of Sasse boys (more than a football team) now in a mixed boarding school like WWMSS Mpundu. The pressure was purely too much for most of Momany's colleagues to bear. Because of the fame from their soccer performance, classroom output, and general Sasse mannerisms, the flocking of the girls was indeed overwhelming and many of his colleagues were torn apart by the choice stage, even before the game proper had actually begun. Most of them were having a taste of it for the first time. On the contrary, backed by the Annastasian and Ritaian experiences in love and understanding, Momany made it academically and otherwise in high-powered gears; and all this happened despite that he had a total replica of Rita there in the person of Susan.

A Charm User. Susan even carried the Ritaian amorous-comportment or lovoldism to higher grounds in the sense that they were in a boarding secondary school with no school and home time like in Rita's case in SHS Fiango. If Rita and Momany were like finger

32

and nail in school, Susan and he simply became each other's oxygen. Even during siesta when she was supposed to be in the girls' dormitory and he in the boys', she would be found hanging around the boys' dormitory; meaning he has to come out and spend that period together with her in a classroom. There were so many love pairs in the school but many of the students just could not comprehend what Momany had done to the Susan they thought they knew well. As mentioned already, the stream of girls was endless and overpowering but Momany had taken his time and chosen Susan because of his *bigimprizism* (love for always going for the big or somewhat impossible prize). That way, he is able to stay focused on just one lover at a time, notwithstanding the distracting and overwhelming rushing flood. Maybe this particular love-skill of Momany should also be attributed to his first teacher or *mandenguelovism*; or is it simply inborn?

I would not want to waste more time on Susan's beauty since Momany's eyes do not see anything that is not outstanding in that domain. She was very mature and off-putting, being widely known in the school and beyond to have nothing to do with "small boys", as she described students and anyone else without a high-sounding title like 'Director', 'Manager' – in short the sugar daddies. Momany seems to have liked her especially as she was not part of the rushing flood in class or school (even as she might also have been dying for him like the rushers). Also perhaps because he knew he would be a Sugar-Daddy killer if he teaches her to love him for him, not just someone's title or money. There was evidently much commotion the day Momany walked up to her desk and, in full view and hearing of all, asked Susan if he could talk to her after class. She herself was apparently taken by surprise and everyone must have been waiting for the explosion and larva to follow when Susan asked for the place of meeting. Momany said it could be anywhere, provided it was before they went to the refectory for lunch. After she said alright, Momany went back to his seat and continued doing what he had been doing as if nothing had just happened; fully aware, of course, of the sensations rippling around.

By the time Momany came out of the dormitory, Susan was already in front of their classroom. He thanked her for coming and they entered into the classroom and sat on one of the back benches. Aware that a lot of people would plant themselves around to eavesdrop on their conversation, Momany had written the following, while still in the dormitory, that he spread out for her to read: "I want us to talk about you and I but since it may involve truths about us that we may not feel comfortable with third parties hearing, I am suggesting that we talk by writing, if you don't mine." When she had read to the end, she approved by nodding. He then wrote: "How would you feel going out with a 'small boy' like me?" Before Momany could push the paper for her to write on, Susan whispered in his ear: "I don't think you're a small boy." He asked why and she whispered again "Because you do not behave like one at all and I love that a lot. You have actually swept me off my feet." Momany had imagined telling her a lot of things during this meeting but the need did not arise. He simply did not quite feel like eating anymore after her fiery kissing and tight embrace that took him completely on the hop. But, as Susan insisted, they headed for the refectory hand in hand. The transformation was so swift and decisive that a lot of the students (particularly those failed eavesdroppers) could not understand how it all happened; with rumours even going around that Momany had "brained" Susan without saying a word. Some 'four-eyes' theorists even went further to say he "had given her charm".

A *Lion-Killer.* Through Susan, Momany's 'lion-killing' skills were also confirmed. When he had told her in December of that school year that he was to visit her at home during Christmas holidays, Susan had objected, saying she would rather come to him. Asked why, she had explained that her dad was a wild lion that would devour any boy that came to their home. Boys in the school from the same town as her had numerously confirmed it, advising Momany not to take that risk at all. But, strong-headed and confident in the domain as he was, he told them to worry about themselves, not about him. The day he arrived at their home and knocked, it was coincidentally Susan's father who attended to the door (perhaps, to 'lion-eat' the stupid prey?). Momany greeted him in a firm tone and introduced himself as Susan's friend from Victoria. He did not at all see the much-talked about lion in this man who very politely asked him in, offered a seat and requested one of his children around to offer Momany a drink and some doughnuts before going to look for Susan who was out, not far.

Susan came in some minutes later and was completely taken aback by the comfortable manner Momany was enjoying himself at the behest of her lion-father who was present at home. There was no embracing and Momany perfectly understood. Susan was still struggling to come to grips that what she was witnessing was real, not a dream. After some hours with the family, Momany announced his departure and her father, who had been in the bedroom most of that time resting, came out to bid him farewell and safe return. Susan accompanied him and they spent another hour or so in town before he boarded a vehicle for Victoria. Susan also joined him in Victoria the next day, still wondering about the happenings of the day before and loving and understanding the 'four-eyes' man even more than before.

A Firstolovist of a Sort: With Susan, Momany also quickly discovered that although she had had many 'big' men in her life before him, Susan had never really loved any person. Momany was thus her first in that respect. This explains why she became so addicted to always being with him; her numerous trips to Yoke during holidays made her another sensation there like Emelda (from Mamfe) before her. In school it was only left for Susan to start spending the nights with Momany in the boys' dormitory; leading a lot of her colleagues or potential rivals to claim and complain that she was not allowing Momany any space and time to study. Her reply was always: "If you think he has to study like us to succeed in anything then you don't know Figaro Cinq [Momany's other nickname that was Susan's favourite] and how his head works." Susan was actually correct because (in spite of all the glamour in WWMSS-Mpundu) Momany was still able to make the G.C.E. Ordinary Level in flying colours while most others, especially in the Sasse troop, failed or had what some education critics usually describe as "four miserable papers at Ordinary Level"; the same glamour and success applying subsequently to Joan and studies at the UNIYAO, as seen in chapter 4 below. All this could be largely attributed to both Momany's very early experiences with Annastasia and Rita and the fact that he never for one minute forgot what he was up to and up against, in so far as concerns his objectives. These goals were palpably threatened in CCAS Kumba. But his spectacular CCAS success came about, largely propped up by the outstanding love and understanding of his very first wife-to-be that never was, *grace à* 99-Sensism?

Chapter 2

A Lot Of Love And Understanding But Spouse-To-Be Transformed Into Spouse-Never-To-Be By 99-Sensism?

The spouse domain is a particular field in which I have always wanted to be better than my father, since it is an area which has been the stronghold of the forces working against and slowing down the advancement in his larger picture outlook on life. Paradoxically, it seems instead to be the one area in which I have had so many failures and un-defining moments that have, without a doubt, curtailed considerably the number of persons that would by now have made their way into "the greatest number of persons possible" whose lives I would already have ameliorated in [unimaginable] ways. [Fossungu, 2013a: 111]

Momany's CCAS Kumba battle had been won through a shortcut, thanks to his then wife-to-be, Anna. But the combat for actually acquiring university education was largely responsible, in a very funny 99-sensical way, for the loss of Anna because the struggle took what has been described as a very unexpected turn, twisting through what appeared to be a hazardously lengthened and meandering double-segment trail (Fossungu, 2013a: 69), with the town of Manjo being at the tail end and also curiously following at the heels of the Yoke Conspiracy against Momany and his wife-to-be. His Manjo stay, as well as the combats and strategies for getting to the UNIYAO in time (that are already discussed in Fossungu, 2013a: chapter 4) could simply be meaningless without a good grasp of Anna whose momentous effect is felt not only on the two Manjo ladies that hastily followed on her own heels for possible replacement but as well on all the others until and after Schola, who eventually became Momany's wife. For now let us see just how central Anna's love and understanding and 99-Sensism have been in Momany's ideal spouse quest.

Is Anna the Beginning and End of Momany's Ideal Spouse Journey?

Anna is Bassa and an undisputable ingredient of academic successes (but of spousal failures?) to Momany. She is not only inseparable from his CCAS Kumba battles and victory, and the Manjo duel for the UNIYAO, etc. She is intertwined too to all the three aspects of the "ideal marriage and family": (1) That the decision to marry be that of the two persons involved, (2) that both parties share a lot in perspectives, and (3) that both parents be there together for the children (see Fossungu, 2013a: chapters 4 & 5). But in this book I will largely tie Anna more to the second factor which relates to this always present need or desire in Momany to have a partner that would share a lot of perspectives with him; resulting from the lessons he learnt from his own father's case especially that he wanted to avoid in his drive to be better than his papa in ameliorating living conditions for "the greatest number of persons possible." From Momany's perceptive, the problems between his father and mother can be summarized as being due to their very contrary ideas of those to help or to consider as children or family. While his papa was a larger picture guy the mother was the narrow picture person (see Fossungu, 2013a: chapters 1 & 2). The bigger picture being described here is not just in connection with financial help. Just imagine the lives of everyone connected to Momany's household if both parents shared similar perspectives, meaning both were looking at the larger picture rather than the narrow.

From Momany's (and other children's) 99-sensism agony catalogued in this book, you will swiftly know some of the deep-seated difficulties that would be engendered by the differing perspectives of a child's parents. That is the foremost reason Momany has always wanted to have as wife someone he could not only easily relate to, in as many fields as possible; but who would also

38

love and understand him as a package and, therefore, what he truly stands for, in spite of the appearances. All those qualities Momany thinks he readily found in Anna, a very natural, deeply thoughtful, and respectful lady who not only converted a Saul to Paul but also loved using letters for communication to a fault. Momany has never really liked his English name(s) being modified in any way;[4] but he is yet to explain why he doesn't seem to worry when his lover(s) do(es) so, as it is plainly done in this chapter. Is that the conversion being talked about then? That we are about to find out; but if Momany's mother (Mami Thecla) could be regarded as the one woman that has greatly impacted on his life by misunderstanding and not appreciating him (Fossungu, 2013a: 7), Anna could be the one of three women having had a similar impact by comprehending and so dearly loving him. The second of five children (three boys and two girls), Anna – I do not quite know how – seemed to have picked it up right that Momany was a man with lots of potentials who needed just real love to be able to have not even the sky being his limit. I put forward this theory because Anna not only came to Momany but did so apparently knowing full well who he was: not only in the domain of girls but also others, including his tribulations at home. In this respect Anna appears to score a big goal over Rita and others for being the first in having the full package from day one.

When (because of those home problems) Momany had made up his mind to sit for the G.C.E. Advanced Level before the usual time and only discussed it with Anna, she was not simply excited and encouraging. She also firmly assured her lover and husband-to-be, who she preferred calling otherwise than Momany: "Piero, I know very well that, with my love wrapped around you as it is, there is nothing you cannot successfully do. I am with you 100%." What else would you demand of a person you are so deeply in love with? Anna was absolutely right and (absent the well calculated blackmail that sort of loosened her love around Momany) no one, in the exact

---

[4] For more on this curious name-modifying phenomenon in Cameroon, see, for example, Fossungu (1997).

words of her 'husband-to-be', "could have succeeded in tearing her away from me while I was still alive." As it then seemed to Momany, they were both in this business together for life. But that was not all there was to her cheering though, for Anna alone found out where Momany usually escaped to, in order to read during the little time he had after farm and before dark. She would often come there to see him, bringing him whatever fruit gifts she could, and leaving almost as soon as she had come, this time not because of the police-like senior brother behind her though. Momany commits to memory once imploring her to stay with him a little longer and Anna's firm response was: "Piero, I come here because I know coming helps your reading and understanding; but I will not be aiding by substantially diminishing the little time you have for that." She gave him the usual goodbye kiss and left.

Anna was always reminding Momany a lot about Annastasia, with the sole and intriguingly contrasting differences being in the former's having a senior sibling and in her being four years younger than Momany. If there had been any lingering doubt at all in Momany's mind (and there was none that he knew of) about succeeding in that examination, it would long have been eradicated by Anna. That is why, on his way from the farm one Saturday in August 1981, Momany was not surprised when a gas station attendant who was unaware that he had sat for the exams indicated that he had heard a name like Momany's over radio as the G.C.E. results were being aired. Celebration or no festivity in their household, Anna and Momany later commemorated it in a very special memorable way in Victoria, far away from Yoke and the nose-pokers. Anna and Momany were both in college when they fell in love but the way she has impacted on his life is comparable only to those of two of his lovers in the primary school years – Annastasia and Rita – as can be picked up from (1) Anna's unique letters and (2) the duo's views on respect and family.

Firstolovism and Annaletterism: Reversing Africa in the West?

Firstolovism describes the act of being in love for the first time. Letters, like their views on respect and on family, are also important indicators to just how much Anna (and/or Schola) and Momany knew each other; had similar perspectives; were ideal for each other for marriage; or otherwise. Much on Schola is not tied only to this part since she effectively became Momany's spouse and thus cuts across everything. This area will therefore have Anna in the driver seat with Schola chairing after in the next chapter with her new definition of family (while in Canada) that excludes spouse and children. Anna and Momany never actually got to the spouse and having children stage but the love they shared was so deep (I guess they would want me to be saying is, not was, because they seem never to have really said goodbye?). That is principally why Momany was ready to fight as much as he could to have this 'life partner' with him while climbing the academic ladder, not after – a combat that took him all the way to Garoua in northern Cameroon and to Sokoto State in Nigeria (see Fossungu, 2013a: chapter 3).

Anna and Momany loved each other so profoundly; yet, it is the deepness of the love they both had for each other that ironically put them where they never for one minute imagined ever finding themselves in – separate lives with third parties and, worse still, on no-speaking terms for close to thirty years. Could the bleak future in Momany during 1981-83 have been overriding in Anna's parents' calculations? And was it because of the deep love that everyone (including her parents) knew to be between them that her parents had to first tear the duo apart through blackmailing Momany to Anna before quickly sending her into marriage with someone in Douala she did not even know? Were the parents here considering the child's best interests or only their own self-centred motives or *scholaparentism*? The authors of the bombshell on Momany's university bid in 1981 (as seen in Fossungu, 2013a: 71-73) knew well that it could not have succeeded without the Dschang legion and schemers.

Was it also obviously clear to Anna's parents that their plot could never have worked without the blackmail?

Explaining the Yoke Conspiracy

In her instructive book, Reaves (1992: 22), tells us that the third goal of science, beyond describing what occurs or predicting what will occur, is to explain something, answering the question, "Why did it happened that way?" To explain something is to give a coherent set of reasons why a particular thing happened as it did and not any other way. Explanation, she carries on, involves finding out the causes, the laws that determine what happens; concluding that theoretical research is particularly useful for testing explanations. So, how do we explicate the happenings in Yoke? As lately expounded to Momany by Anna's mother, the Yoke Blackmail happened because of what Zembylos (2013: 20) could call "Ethnic estrangement". That is to say that Anna's father did not like her daughter marrying Momany because of his dislike of Bangwa people (the outside arm of 99-Sensism); with the rest of them in the family not being able to say otherwise since "we were all very afraid of him."

This explanation is not only questionable but also carries a lot to be desired. Most importantly, it raises the question of the love and understanding between Anna's parents (to leave out parents-children), with this questionability stemming from the indicated fear of the man even by his own wife. Questions are raised. Would male dominance in marital unions in Africa be directly or indirectly responsible for the attitude of most African women in the Western world? In other words, is it because of their excessive starvation of equal status in the union there that pushes most of these women to exaggerate on 'equality' when they find themselves in Western societies that preach equal status? By 'exaggerating on equality' I simply mean to describe the fact that these women, while in the said societies, do not seem to see the need for equality but rather the urgent and unthinking need for reversing Africa in the West; or, as some critics put it, they want to become the African men and make the African men the African women in the West. Whatever the case

42

with the Africa-West reversing women, just do not hurry to be one of those who hastily picks up a lone 'bad' thing from a minuscule part or culture of Africa and make a general rule of it. I could not find any better condemnation for the attitude than that of Reaves (1992: 29) who states that "Another case of faulty conclusions from casual thinking is our tendency to draw false generalizations from specific observations. When you have had contact with one or a few members of a group, there is a tendency to think all members of the group are similar to the ones you have met. Many social stereotypes are born this way."

Don't therefore conclude here in particular that African men *always* dominate in marriage unions. You are advised to patiently hang on until you later meet the contrasting parents of a Manjo girl called Elizabeth who (following very closely on Anna's heels with a conspicuous brandishing of her questionable 'Anglophone Card') also found a long-sought unique husband in Momany. Before we later reach Manjo, a graphical issue to resolve in regard of the invisible hand behind Anna's parents' own *scholaparentism* by way of the conspiracy is: Why didn't Anna's mom's explanation on her husband's hatred of 99-sensers privately come when Momany was then on his knees begging for her help in the matter? The explanation concerning Anna's father's anti-Bangwaness, coming after the man's death, is very hard to sell though. Could Anna's dad's position on Bangwa be convincing, especially in view of his very cordial comportment towards Momany until then? Should one not be tempted to think that the conspiracy all had to do with the guy's apparent dead-end future at the time? Is this dead-end fact not due also to a version of the inside arm of 99-Sensism in the household itself? Does it import then that, either way, 99-sensism cannot be put out in the Anna Affair?

Momany knew then that there was foul play somewhere but Anna could not and did not figure this out, maybe, because of her firstolovism or act of being in love for the first time? Because she was so mad about what she had been told by the two Banyangi women (her parents' cohorts, it is said)? Could it be by mere coincidence (or is it a well designed choice) that these ladies are of the ethnic group whose own popular epithet in Cameroon for its females is *ashawo* or prostitutes? Whatever the case, their concocted story or conversation was that Momany had lately been regularly sleeping with each of them; exquisitely 'doing papa and mama' to them like no other man they had ever known. Wow! The two ladies (Yoke tenants of Momany's papa, for that matter) actually made it look like Anna was only overhearing them 'accidentally'. Perfecto! As Anna and Momany were no longer on the same side, both war and battle were woefully lost by both of them; but Momany particularly when he got Anna's last brutally piercing letter telling him off and giving him all the freedom in the world to "forget about me and continue sleeping around with your Banyangi harlots." As Momany jokingly but still very painfully put it many years later, "Since I did not die when Anna was manipulated out of my life, I am certain I would not die without having carried my objective to a higher level and platform." Was it the expert design of the plot or did Anna easily fall into the manoeuvrings because of her prior knowledge of Momany's past with women? Was her comportment after the blackmail consonant with someone who loved and understood Momany the way he says she did? In other words (and also drawing from Chantal's fascinatingly instructive case to be seen later in chapter 4's Chantadelamatism), could it really be that a love as deep as this cannot withstand conniving pressures from the outside? Or, is it largely because dialogue or one-on-one discussion was put behind monologue or letter communication?

Dialogue over Monologue

Anna and Momany were as real and committed lovers as anyone could imagine; but could Anna's comportment be explained in terms of her untruthfulness, or of the bitterness that blinded her from seeing the need for dialogue, or of the policing attitude of her senior sibling that could have pushed her to put dialogue behind monologue? Letters are a kind of monologue that may be good when the ride is smooth but do not seem to aid matters when the road gets bumpy. For example, after a sentence, there is no possibility for the other party to interject or correct anything you have said or even slow down the anger; and, therefore, you just keep pouring everything out before sending to the other. And you will not be there either to listen to that other. Perhaps, with love and understanding problems like these people should rather talk one on one (as Momany did with Schola in the 'out of marriage' children tale in chapter 3 below) than use letters?

Truth is obviously bitter but where love and understanding exist the bitter truth has to be told and embraced; and that is perhaps what makes love and understanding the formidable force to the success of the union. One of such bitter hindsight truth is obviously that Momany justly never foresaw what was then happening to his ideal relationship with Anna and reasonably tried all he could humanly do to have a dialogue with Anna but she was adamant. His going on kneels to her mother for her to beg Anna to at least talk to him even seemed to have worsened his case – he was unaware that he was jumping from frying pan to fire, as it is said. If only Anna had given Momany the chance to explain to her what he then suspected was going on! If only Anna had emulated Annastasia (who astutely refused to believe lies about Momany from his own sister, as seen in the Pregnancy Story's *Sistelovism* in the next chapter)! But Anna's anger against Momany, it would seem, had overpowered her love for him. That is precisely one of the important messages or lessons I am trying (through Momany's tale) to pass on here to others: when you become bitter, it is your (bitter) emotion that rules your reasoning rather than your reasoning ruling as it should. Could that not be the same problem with Schola?

On Momany's part, he did not let anything get out of hand, not even his cherished love for Anna. Indeed, then twenty-three, Momany was incapacitated for several weeks, if not months and years, since the very shoulders he had grown so used to deriving his invincible force from in such trying circumstances were no longer accessible to him. Beatrice, his sister, especially did her best to help Momany out but anything short of Anna herself was not as helpful.

This Momany guy, of course you already know that, had been so deeply in love before; but with this Anna woman it was just something else, a beloved wife from the moment he read her first bold love letter.

A Love letter Like No Other

As I said earlier, Anna knew Momany so well in the girls-domain when she came to him using a love letter. In a lot of ways Anna's love letter to him was not just like other love letters he had been used to receiving or himself writing. It was not just the usual somewhat flattering "your running nose provides my butter" stuff. Furthermore, Momany was until then used to most girls just giving the signs on which he followed up, if interested. But here was someone actually, for the first time (by way of letters!) and unexpectedly, professing her deep love for him; and this was being done even before he had told her himself (nor even by any sign at all) that 'I love you'. It was simply touching, ecstatic. From the unpleasant Alice episode in early 1975 in the Victoria school (see Charalicism in chapter 1), Momany knows very well what the risks involved in this kind of love letter are. You can thus see the risk that Anna was taking by writing the distinctive letter that transformed an apparently wayward Saul to a devout Paul; she being, moreover, a younger girl the guy had been meeting but had never looked at in terms of a lover. Wasn't he opening his four-eyes wide enough here too?

Perhaps, as some would say, when you are the centre of everyone's attention you often fail to see those who really love you for you, and not for the attention pulling. And since not many are as bold and truthful as Anna to device any means by which to go straight ahead for what they really want, many stories like this one do not get the chance to be told. I do not know if this theory could also explain why various stars are finding it so hard having a real and lasting relationship; the experts have that over to them. But one thing I know very well is that Momany found her comportment to be too bold of "little" Anna and it certainly stroke the right note in his soul:

an unmistakable indication of someone who knew exactly what she wanted and was not afraid to go for it; just the perfect woman for him as a wife, he told himself, and the AAD instantly switched on, shutting out all the myriad of attention-seekers (including even sensational Susan?).

Momany cannot tell just how many times he read that love note when Anna herself hand-delivered it to him. But every time he was doing so a small clear voice in him kept mocking him (why haven't you seen her before as your future wife?) while he was melting into her bold love like salt does in a pot of hot delicious soup. In his exact words, "If I still had that fateful love letter (I destroyed it and others in 1994 after marrying Schola), I would have liked you to put it verbatim to your readership because it was a classic love note, also jammed with a lot of counselling." Essentially, he says, Anna opened it with "My Dear Piero", followed immediately with condemning Momany's waste of energy and useful time with girls that were not at all deserving of him; indicating how some of them (from a certain ethnic group – Banyangi) were nothing but the prostitutes that she thought they were.[5] Anna then narrowed her lecture or counsel to herself and Momany, introducing self briefly before telling him how she was a very special girl that (in spite of the unending pressures from several boys and men, flashing lots of this and that to win her) had cautiously preserved herself and virginity especially for only one precious guy that she found Momany to be.

---

[5] At the time of Anna's entrance, the only woman in Momany'a life was Susan (from North West – Noni), who was also widely known in Yoke. Of course, there is always this confusion that Momany (who is a sort of every lady's man?) actually would be dating all the attention-seeking women. You will shortly see this also in Manjo in the thinking of Christine and of Elizabeth. In a way (from Momany's perspective), this perception is double-sided like Momany's likeability itself because, an obvious disadvantage that it seems to be, he thinks it is also a good barometer for knowing those who truly love him for who they know he is, including his 'defect' (of being every woman's man) that is already known to and understood by them. Momany may think what he likes here but doesn't it greatly open the room for the easy success of plots like the Yoke one under discussion now?

Anna, to Momany, was indeed a first in almost all aspects, except that she was not the first virgin he was then meeting. "But her way of making me know why she thought I deserved to be the one to have her virginity made her a first. Another first (quite apart from her being the first to ever come across my mind from day one as wife material) was the way this girl was so mature in love though being a first time lover." It is somewhat very hard to elucidate on how a novice could be that expertly in love matters than some long-standing experienced lovers. Are there many such fields in life that do not quite require prior expertise for expert performance? Of course, it is obvious that this could not be Maher's case of "stealing with the eyes" which was imperative for novices because the apprenticeship system was structured to prevent them from "acquiring the whole trade" (Prentice, 2012: 406). Prentice's study examines the relationship between knowledge practices, skill acquisition, and the constitution of economic selfhood in Trinidad, drawing on 15 months of ethnographic fieldwork (from 2003 to 2004), including nine months of participation observation on the shop floor of a local garment factory (*id*: 401). The two fields are thus not the same and, as you will discover, the expert-novice question has not been provoked in this book by just Anna's fisrtolovist maturity; many other Momany-discovered firstolovists exhibit it as well. But Anna's case was simply incredible and Momany thought the good Lord had wonderfully spared him the long search for a life partner, especially if respect remains reciprocal.

Annaspectism and the Reciprocal Nature of Respect

The growth of these two deeply-in-love youths toward the life partner status was however somehow frigid due mostly also to the hostile, policing, and disrespectful attitude of Anna's senior brother. This guy also reminded Momany very much of another direct senior brother of yet another pre-Anna Bangwa Yoke virgin called Agnes. Like Anna, Agnes was a student of Cameroon Baptist Academy in Muyuka but (unlike Anna who was a day student) she was a boarding student; otherwise, Momany would never have had any chance to be seeing her. As sweet, lovely and deeply in love with Momany as she was, Agnes was so frightened of her senior brother that she would not even look at Momany, let alone smile, if she passed by in the company of said brother. An extreme form of janodilism, isn't it? It was plainly ridiculous and it is pretty clear that these policing guys, if they had their way, would also have intimidated Momany away from their sisters. Could it then be that guys like Momany who have had the chance to date many girls (other people's sisters) naturally cultivate this habit of treating their own sisters (as well as their boyfriends) with due respect? If that is the case, how then can Momany's brother's (Joseph's) approach, for example, also be explained? Maybe Momany's conversations with both sister and girlfriend could help in the matter?

Conversations with Beatrice and with Christine

Beatrice is one of Momany's junior sisters and Christine is his lover in Manjo but the conversations he had with both of them addresses the issues of respect and fear in very impressive manners; as well as exposing Christine's intriguing education (styled *christickinology*) on these questions, an instruction that Momany thinks would simply put Christine in a class of her own. I will begin with Beatrice and her boyfriend, followed by Christine and her theorization on respectful boldness.

Beatrice and Boyfriend

Not being the type that goes around nosing for information about people generally and his brothers and sisters particularly, Momany once stumbled on Beatrice and her boyfriend. The way she disappeared in thin air kind of surprised him; he immediately saw janodilism and/or annaspectism (or one-sided respect). Some days later, Momany had to sit his junior sister down and inquired why she did that. Brother, she explained, it was out of respect. Fear or respect, he asked. Beatrice seemed not to see any difference between the two as she pursued: "When my senior brother 'catches' me with a boy, I

49

think the respectful thing to do is to quickly take off." My dear Beatrice, her brother said, "I want you to listen to me very carefully. First, I do not 'catch' anyone since I do not police you, to begin with. I have told you and the others several times that I do not like people (especially my brothers and sisters) being afraid of me because, when that is the case, we cannot usually have a fruitful conversation." Second, Momany pursued, respect is a two-way street, not one-way; meaning that it is reciprocal or give and take; not give and give and give.

He then told Bea that the respectful thing she should have done was to have introduced her friend to him, not to run away the way she did. Beatrice seemed not to have believed that she heard her brother properly, so Momany repeated what he had just said; adding that it also, among other things, puts the boyfriend on guard, if he should go messing around. Giving him a big hug, Bea simply said "I just wish all my brothers were like you, not like that wild beast [referring, of course, to Joseph]." But before Momany could go Bea asked, almost prophetically: "But, Brother, don't you think doing as you have said could also open up my boyfriend and I to blackmail?" Momany admitted it was a possibility, but cautioning all the same that "those who intend to blackmail you would still do so, whether or not you have formally introduced your lover to us." Momany could be quite right in a way because Anna, for instance, never formally introduced him to anyone in her family but that still did not stop the blackmail.

With another sister of Momany, no such introduction had also been made of her classmate at the UNIYAO and he only knew the exact nature of their relationship the day the guy had sustained some wounds on the ear from his sister's bite. Even then, Momany did not ask any nose-poking questions but simply took the suffering man (who had also become his friend through association) to hospital, then purchased his medicines out of pocket and dropped him off. Of course, both lovers greatly respected Momany, not only as their lecturer, but from that day their respect and awe for him multiplied ten-fold. This talk of respect between teacher and students, and of

50

love and understanding, can clearly not pass on without Christine's invaluable lessons on respectful boldness.

Lessons in Christickinology: Christine and Respectful Boldness

Momany met Christine in early 1984 in Manjo where he was then teaching. She is a tall and well-built light-skinned splendour with a uniquely charming way of walking (that very strikingly resembles Anna's) and having this air of retention about her that is kind of very standoffish and menacing. Her seemingly unapproachable composure obviously quickly drew Momany to her but he got really hooked once he got to know and be with her. Amazingly, Christine was already so profoundly in love with him before his approaching her but was keeping her cool; being magically aware that Momany would "soon come home to me." Her exposition of the point, in Momany's view, clearly made her a first in a matchless way. As she killed Momany off with her explanation, "I have never before loved any person, which explains why I am still a virgin. But I do not know how it happened, knowing only that I fell instantly in love with you when I saw you." Was this Rita in the school in Kumba all over again, but without the bold ways? But why were you not bold enough to come and tell me that, Momany asked Christine. "Sir, do you too seriously think I am shy?" He said he did not think so then but wondered what would have happened if he too did not approach her. It is not the same, she rejoined. How and why different, he wanted to know.

Christine looked at him hard (and he did not then seem to recognize her because "love, they say, can change anything, everything",[6] including her unfriendly poise that had already vanished) and then said: "Are you sure you don't just want me to explain something you already know?" As a teacher, Momany reminded her, "I have come to know that repetition sometimes results in better understanding." As if diverting from the point of discussion, Christine commented: "I have never really taken English

---

[6] I am adopting the phrase here from the Nigerian movie, *Worlds Apart*.

seriously but that has drastically changed since your arrival." Recalling his own experience with mandenguelovism in the Yoke school, Momany pondered if she was sure she was not confusing her love for the messenger for his message? Christine intelligently agreed that it may be true but went on to shrewdly distinguish: "I have fallen for you not because you are teaching English but I am sure your way of teaching it has made many of us to come to like the subject" (also cited in Fossungu, 2013a: 132). Momany was then wondering. Did this lady somewhat prepare both this meeting and topics of discussion or is it just that when you are bold and truthful you have no reason to struggle with your words and ideas? He was very much enjoying Christine's sapient conversation and did not let her get away with the 'how and why different' lecture that she had hoped was already forgotten.

"You see, Sir," she began, but he had to cut in and requested her replacement of Sir with his first name and she duly thanked him, saying she knew from day one that she would learn a lot from him; and he added that he too was doing the same from her, asking her to continue. But (like Susan in WWMSS-Mpundu), Christine swiftly altered her position and, before Momany knew it, instead kissed him so hard and long that "I do not think I quite remembered where we were and what we were discussing when it was all over. She absolutely nailed the truth home with that miraculous kiss." Mesmerized as he was, Momany simply told Christine that her kissing was magical and she was glad, indicating that it was her very first. How come then she could do it that well? This really resembles, if not actually, Paulo Freire's "Learning to Do It by Doing It" (Weis and Fine, 2013: 232). It is also largely supported by Christine's response to the question: "Chéri, I just did it. Perhaps, it is as pleasant as you say because it is not only true and respectfully bold but also coming straight from my heart to yours. You deserve it because you have awakened it." With the last sentence especially, Momany's mind instantly flashed back to MTU Girl and he was pondering if he could have done same or better to that woman who roused his love, if he had had the unique opportunity. But MTU Girl was long out of the picture and it was Christine that was there and then giving him her all in the domain of love and understanding; and truly making Momany to kind of seriously wonder if Anna was simply as irreplaceable as he had imagined.

Momany used to marvel at Anna's intelligence but Christine was here truly baffling him with the depth of her own penetration. Chéri, she continued, "I am not timid as most people erroneously think; I simply know the difference between rushing boldness and respectful boldness." As Momany explained off his awe for christickinology, he once wrote an essay on discipline during an examination in form three in Sasse College and his English tutor (an Englishman – R.W. Musker) commented that he had thought he knew much on the subject until he read Momany's paper. Similarly, Momany went on, he too had thought he knew quite a lot on boldness but Christine's here was kind of new to him even if he did not want to interrupt her for another distinction with one still pending. "Since you came around," Christine, apparently and intelligently reading Momany's mystified mind, pursued, "almost every girl in school has been running around after you. Now Chéri, would you have been able to visualize just how different I am from the pack if I was also running around for you like them?" The overwhelmed man had to concur he might not have, and she concluded that "I therefore count myself very lucky to know that the first and only man I love this much also loves me." To his instinctive question why she was so sure that he loved her, without hesitation, Christine said "Because only pure love could have brought you to me (even as I was dying for you) at a moment when you were already having the sex that most men are often after with those many girls scrambling for you." Flashing quickly back at his love life till that very moment, all Momany could then hear himself saying was "Isn't this really something?"

If he had indeed gone to her just to explore, Momany was now completely drowned in Christine's wise and respectfully bold love. Her wisdom brought many thoughts flashing back to him. For example, could it be because Momany had failed to make the distinction (between rushing and respectful boldness) in the 'cockler

53

(or girls-winning) lessons' to him that his brother, Joseph, was wont to unexpectedly bring home any girl he had succeeded in *cocklering* and, in full view of all, including their mother, get into their room (the boys' room in Yoke was directly opposite mum's and the girls'), ask out any of them he found in, lock up and have his sexual satisfaction? But then, Momany wondered, would Joseph be bold and truthful if he pretended to be what (respectful) he was clearly not? Momany can still recall Joseph's response when he once asked him if he did not think doing so was very disrespectful to mum especially: "Is it her that does not also have sex?" In short, that initial conversation with Christine was having effects comparable to Anna's bold love letter and Momany could not stop wondering why Christine was not the first or only girl in Manjo that he had gone out with.

Whether or not the Manjo strategies and roadblocks to university education had anything to do with the fact that Christine did not become Momany's wife (as elaborated on in subsequent chapters), here is a little talk of what I think about this one-way 'respect' or annaspectism. I am then tempted to be drawn to this feeling that boys/girls who are so hostile to seeing someone date their sisters/brothers are either losers in front of other girls/boys or they are just being damned stupid. Momany clearly told Anna something similar to this while also giving her another more refined version of the conversation with his own sister, Beatrice. But Anna seems to have refused to see the need for turning her respect for her senior brother into a reciprocal affair, defending her stance to Momany in the following terms: "My beloved Piero, I know my brother well. I love you very much but that should not mean I shouldn't have a continued good relationship with my brother." Was Momany convinced then? Not really; but he knew as well that any healthy relationship had to be graced with the give and take idiom (not the take and take and take one that is tenaciously embraced by the wife he eventually ended up with, as seen in the next chapter) and so he had then given acquiescence: notwithstanding that (either way) this one-way respect stance was eventually to convert a wife-to-be to a wife-never-to-be.

From Wife-to-Be to Wife Never-to-Be

Momany nevertheless only grasped the full repercussions of Anna's reasoning or annaspectism about sixteen years later, when he was doing postgraduate studies at the UNIYAO. That is, when he had met equally beautiful Odilia, who could be flawlessly described as Anna's replica. A virgin then as well, Odilia was the junior sister of a very good friend of Momany's (as he used to think) and the perfect match and ideal replacement for Anna; having the additional bonuses of being Bangwa and a graduate of Saker Baptist College in Victoria – the female version of Sasse College, his alma mater. Not only also very unpretentious, deeply unselfish and reverential, and having almost the same physique with Anna, Odilia (for some strangely coincidental reasons) also preferred calling him Pierrot like Anna. Wasn't this just like finding some very precious thing that you had lost before? The answer to this important question will be attempted with (1) janodilism from the Saker Baptist College (SBC) girls and (2) Elizabeth and the Anglophone Card.

Janodilism and the Saker Baptist College (SBC) Girls

Janodilism, another form or synonym of annaspectism, is already familiar from the last chapter and is clearly exhibited in and by the two SBC ladies behind it, one of whom is Odilia. Very highly intelligent and always willing to learn, Odilia too was great joy just being around Momany's being. He basically saw in her the coming back of Anna in another way and practically did not want to waste any moment before marrying her. He therefore let her know one day that he intended to break the exciting news of their engagement to her senior sister, his friend, who was then also studying in the UNIYAO. Like Anna, Odilia advised against the idea, stressing also that she knew her senior sister very well and that this 'news breaking' could wait until the time was ripe.

55

But Momany did not quite comprehend her then, not seeing what the problem of ripe time was since (as was with Anna) he had already convinced himself from day one that Odilia was the one and he was never out to just play around with her and thought it was only normal for the sister – also an SBC graduate – to be formally informed of their plan to get married. Momany has till date regretted however not having taken the advice of his wife-to-be because the bizarre attitude of her senior sister (whom Odilia "respected" almost religiously) thereafter turned Odilia quickly and determinedly into his wife-never-to-be. There is usually the belief in many African family circles that when a junior sister in the family gets married before her seniors, the latter would hardly be able to find their own husbands. Could Odilia's sister's comportment be tied to this popular saying within some family circles, or to something else? Why did Momany not listen to Odilia or even reluctantly complied like he did with Anna? Can it be because the former did not go ahead to further explicate her case in like manner as the latter?

By the way, Anna had emphasized to Momany in propping up her point on her police-like sibling, "you have me for life and I see nothing to worry about him who will very soon not be there." His immediate reaction was "Will your brother soon die?" Anna coolly said: "I know you do not mean that; but your funny sense of humour is one of the countless things that really get me hooked on you." Yes, indeed, many people have always said that to Momany before (and continue saying so till date, including Odilia); but he admits it always has a different feeling when it is coming from Anna. Momany also recalls his nickname of 'Power' also assuming a different and more intimately special connotation when Schola started using it in 1994 after their honeymoon in Yaoundé (where she discovered the name, as it was the name everyone there was using). I guess that is exactly what happens when you are really in love? But can this love survive where fear for parents, siblings, and other acquaintances is equated with respect?

It is known that Momany believes that serious relationships (leading to marriage) have to begin between the two people concerned before reaching their various families. When Odilia was in the University in Nigeria (far away from her controlling senior sister) and he was in Alberta, they resumed friendly communications. Back from Edmonton in November 1992 and residing in Douala, Odilia too had returned earlier and was working in Buea where she was still single and still living with her parents. Momany earnestly wanted to have a serious discussion with her to find out if she was still interested in their getting married. I cannot enumerate enough the many trips the man-in-love made to Buea for the purpose, with Odilia always having one reason or another to put the discussion or meeting off. Thrice or twice Momany was even at their home with his father but there the matter always ended because Odilia and he had not settled on the issue as yet. Was her senior sister still running her life or what?

Odilia's parents knew Momany well and must have sensed that there was something very serious about those visits (even leaving out the two or three in the company of his dad). But how could Momany have let the cat out of the bag again without Odilia's full green light? Because of his belief in this decision emanating first from the two people concerned, Momany let the Odilia-cat stay where it preferred and moved on; knowing full well that if he overstepped again, Odilia would be completely entitled to comport herself like earlier in Yaoundé; an attitude that inevitably led Momany to a wife whose parents instead seem to have cast a spell on her. The case of parental spell on Schola can be clearly picked up in the next chapter from how central they had long ago become in Schola's calculations and whole being to the total exclusion of the children and Momany.

But parental and sibling spell would not be all there is to the point. Take also the case of Jane, a Dschang lady, to demonstrate the case of the spell of or fear for acquaintances. Jane is another ex-student of SBC like Odilia; a very sweet and wonderful lady but for this fear or "religious respect" thing or janodilism. At the time Momany met Jane she was in the graduation year at the UNIYAO but he has never regretted his not having Jane as his wife as much as his not having her parents and siblings as his in-laws. When Jane had introduced Momany to them, it was so welcoming and warm. It was even beyond description when Momany also went there one day in 1990 with his own father who had arrived in Yaoundé to "chase" the *dossier* for his retirement benefits. It was simply looking like a perfect meeting of in-laws, as unplanned as it was. Good supportive parents and siblings are important but not all that would matter in this matter. Some people do have these types of parents/siblings but do not still succeed since they do lack other qualities like knowing what they want and who they are; short, being bold and truthful in love – lovoldism.

Jane clearly had all going for her but could not seem to get a grip of herself largely because of her fear of her seniors ("bigs") in SBC. Some people might want to jump to critiquing single-sex colleges but I think it will be rushing too fast to wrong conclusions or "Unscientific Empiricism" (Reaves, 1992: 28-29), especially – to even leave Momany's own case aside – as bold and truthful Emelda was from one of such schools known as Okoyong in Mamfe. It might principally be a matter of personality. Momany well recalls one day that he was with Jane and she suddenly vanished like Beatrice, his sister. He did not know why but Jane later explained that she had not wanted a senior in SBC that she knew Momany once briefly dated to see her with him. Is this not janodilism at its extreme? What could be more mulovundistically ridiculous than that? And is this in regard of just one particular 'big'?

Jane was living in the same street as Momany and all seemed to be moving on so smoothly towards marriage until one weekend evening when he made one of the usual visits to her parents'. He had been there for a while and had seen everyone else except Jane and inquired if she was not yet in. Surprise was written all over the faces of all. It was her father who broke the seemingly endless silence with "You are not aware that Jane is out of town and in Douala with her 'big'?" Momany was as dumbfounded as everyone but managed to hold himself together and simply said: "There must be some small misunderstanding somewhere." Returning home that night, he could not sleep. He was already such a part of Jane's family that he scarcely

58

can find the appropriate words to put on. A thousand things crossed his mind. Who was this 'big' of hers and what was being cooked up? Why did Jane not inform him of her trip? Where are the love and understanding? If it was so urgent, why did she not even scribble a fast note and drop at his place (that she passes by) on her way to the main street where she boards a taxi? Her response later to the last question was that the big was in a hurry and she could not afford to "disobey" her. Momany could not bring himself to understand this weird behaviour especially viewing what he considers as Jane's advantages over the others like Anna in particular.

Whatever the actual case with Anna's parents' reasoning for the flop with her, both of Jane's parents are okay, even brothers and sisters. Jane is also the only one who had somewhat been formally presented to Momany's own dad. Unlike Anna, Jane has language (with Momany's birth mother who does not speak English or French or Pidgin) on her side like Odilia. Jane is also in a family of five siblings like Anna but, unlike Anna, she is the first – no big brother/sister to police her. Despite all what had happened with the Douala Trip Momany pardoned Jane and especially wanted to tell the whole world during his send-off party (to the University of Alberta) in August 1991 that Jane was the one he was marrying. But she did not show up in spite of the invitation and insistence that she be there. Obtaining her parents' permission for the occasion, of course, was a non-issue. Did she fail to come perhaps because she foresaw some of her SBC seniors or 'bigs' also being there? Momany even wrote to Jane from Edmonton asking about her life and she blew everything then because (like Odilia) she was suffering from *nonoselfism*, meaning she did not appear to know herself and what she really wanted in life. Both of these janodilistic SBC girls are very unlike Elizabeth who was very lovoldistically (boldly in love and) ready to follow her heart, with or without her parents' approval.

Lectures in Lovanglocardism: Elizabeth and the Anglophone Card

To some experts, demographic categories are historic, structural, social, psychological, embodied, and fictional. But they cannot simply be theorized away (Weis and Fine, 2013: 226). Welcome to Manjo and to the Anglophone/Francophone Confusion in Cameroon which clearly would provide "a space where critical ethnographers might address the complex choices we engae as we analyze narrative material that at times justifies existing applications, reifies individualism, or seems to work against class, gender, and/or racial/ethnic self-interests" (Weis and Finer, 2013: 224). This is no idle talking on mine or those specialists' part because the concepts or categories of 'Anglophone' and 'Francophone' have been so politicized and twisted in Cameroon that they most often have no sensible meaning; being employed in situations that are very far from those that they actually should be referring to (see Fossungu, 2013c: 84-87). For example, some like Elizabeth here would seem to think that the mere fact of residing in the former West Cameroon or the English-speaking Regions of North West and of South West (what Fossungu (2013c: 4) respectively calls Savannazone and Debundschazone) makes you an Anglophone.

Anglophone or not, Elizabeth does not only follow on Anna's heels; she also flamboyantly reminds Momany a lot about Anna, not only because she too was a virgin when he met her. She also kind of gravitated to him like Anna (though in person and not through letter). Still under the smacking of the Yoke Conspiracy, Momany had just arrived in Manjo on Wednesday 21 September 1983 to take up a teaching appointment with Collège de l'Unité de Manjo. He had the position and was asked by the principal to teach until Friday before running to the South West during the weekend to bring up his belongings. In the meantime, through a conspicuous '*Chambre À Louer*' display, he had already taken up an empty available room in a house directly opposite the college and had retired there at noon that first day, waiting for the afternoon session. It was very hot and the only window of the room that opens directly to the college was wide open, with the door closed but not locked. He was not asleep (there was even no bed to be falling asleep on) and could thus see when this Rita-like very beautiful ebony black young lady came to the window. She greeted him, smiling very charmingly and broadly, and Momany answered but was not sure he knew what her business there was, although recognizing (from her uniform) that she was a student from the college. She had this sizable bag containing all sorts of fruits that was meant for him. Momany was really wondering if this was not Anna again together with his reading (now teaching) hide-out in Manjo.

Elizabeth was not looking uncomfortable at all at the window but still asked if Momany would not be kind and gentlemanly enough to let her in. He told her the door was not locked and she came in. Her beauty, of course, was not in any doubt but it was her confidence and comfortable manners that immediately caught his attention then. At this point, most African (or to be specific, Anglophone Cameroonian) girls would think they have given you more than enough signs or leads, expecting you to continue from there. Not Elizabeth. She boldly took the lead, speaking in fluent English (for a Cameroon-Francophone). Sounding very much like Anna, she warned Momany about all those other useless girls in class who do not measure up to the task [he was pondering about the 'task'] and would certainly only create scandals for him if he is not careful. The young newly love-beaten man was already posing questions in his mind on the relevance of her class. Like Anna again, Elizabeth then narrowed down almost instinctively and introduced herself as a very different and special girl who has for so long been idealizing a husband whose hard-to-describe picture she thought Momany completely fit. She did not fail to emphasize in the typical Cameroon-Francophone style (of regarding all Anglophones as brothers and sisters, and who only stick to themselves) that she was Momany's "Anglophone sister" from Kumba.[7]

---

[7] It is dealt with later (in chapter 4) but I must have to emphasize here that the ethnic or cultural group of a person does not appear to have ever been a factor that

61

Elizabeth was very bold and truthful, no doubt. She said so many good things about "us Anglophones" in making her case why she, but not any of the others in her Francophone class or school (that "were just ready to devour you and pass on") merited being his wife. But Momany was not paying much attention to that; instead greatly wondering if she had previous knowledge of Anna and what he had just been through in Yoke – because there were too many similarities between the two of them to require detailing out. But it is the contrast in their situations that really stroke the cord so hard. While it was Anna's father who supposedly did not like Momany's "Bangwaness" (outside arm of 99-Sensism), it was instead Elizabeth's mother who did not like him on that score. Momany commits to memory when Elizabeth first introduced him to her parents the following December at their home in Kumba. Her dad and the young man snapped in as soon as they met; discussing any subject as if they were not only pals but had also known each other a very long time. In short, from a few questions of his, Momany knew he was more than ready to gladly welcome Momany's "knock-door" for the hand of his daughter, with whom he cracked a lot of jokes even in Momany's presence. The young man saw a perfect father-in-law in Elizabeth's father. But his wife was the reverse, making it no secret that a Bangwa could only marry her daughter over her dead body; and even hushing anyone, including her husband, who thought otherwise.

The 99-Sense Theory has certainly done a lot of harm to Momany. But Caution! Do not rush to talking great failure or harm until chapter 3. There you will encounter what happened when Momany actually married a 99-sense person like himself: The much more destructive inside arm of parental 99-sensism would then take its toll, surprisingly transforming his much cherished love and understanding into one-sided love, complications and sabotage. Does

---

Momany considers in terms of selecting a lover or spouse, his main idea being on the person's boldness and truthfulness, backed by his/her larger picture way of looking at life. So what must have gone wrong with bold and truthful Elizabeth in Manjo?

all this easily happen most probably because Momany does not exhibit the 99-sensism he is being feared for by the non-99-sensical parents? Most often some parents act or react without in the least appreciating what their conduct could lead the children into. It is without a doubt obvious that Elizabeth did not like her mother's highhandedness and (very unlike Anna, Odilia, Jane, and Schola) was ready to follow her heart, with or without the approval of her mum especially. I get this impression from what Momany says happened when he was leaving. Elizabeth's mother did not even want her to accompany him an inch and when Elizabeth disagreed and insisted on seeing her lover off, she accorded her just five minutes. Her daughter openly "rebelled" and went all the way to where Momany was spending the night, planning to stay till the next morning. When Momany advised that she should not exaggerate, she tearfully countered: "Fiancé, I am sorry. I just don't know what has come over my mother today. It is not like they did not know that my fiancé was coming home today. Bangwa or no Bangwa, I don't care! It is me and not her that want to marry the husband I have chosen. What actually does she find wrong with your being Bangwa?" This girl's question certainly brings to the foreground what Zembylos (2013: 20) sees as "the complexities and unexpected (dis)connections between children's experiences and the lived experiences of those [parents] whose stories were heard."

It could be that Elizabeth's mother has had some nasty "experiences" with a Bangwa person but never knew of Momany's ethnic group until Momany's discussion with the girl's father during which the issue popped up. Elizabeth too must not have been able to acquaint her parents with that information beforehand, not just because she does not care about Momany's ethnicity; but most probably because of the general Francophone mannerism of often regarding 'Anglophones' as an ethnic group, often distinguishing between them (if they do at all) only with the two regions (North-West & South-West). Zembylos' (2013: 20) article helps to highlight the potential of teaching about/for empathy and "asks what sort of pedagogy can encourage the development of empathy in children who grew up in conflicting societies and are often assigned the burden of 'remembering' unlived memories, that is, events they have not experienced firsthand." Elizabeth seems to be one of such children and, as to what the "lived memories" of Elizabeth's mother were, Momany did not know that himself but tried to let Elizabeth know that her staying the night might have to also put off the father who was on their side. She saw with him and agreed to return home; vowing nonetheless to run away with him if it had to come to that. But was Momany equally ready to lead her on? We shall find that out in the next chapter, including a detailed look in chapter 4 at the equally interesting case of Chantal who Momany was very ready and even rushing to lead on to marriage but paradoxically became the most indecisive at decision time. Could children, one-sided love, and africanscience actually have had a hand in these unusual marriage occurrences?

Chapter 3

Children, Marriage, One-Sided Love and Understanding, and the Reconceptualization of 'Family' In Canada: Africanscience Involvement?

When we engage ethnographically, speak to people in interviews or focus groups, and collect simple descriptive survey data as linked to a more broad-based ethnographic project, it is important to acknowledge that individuals and/or collectivities, no matter how positioned, are trying to make sense – knowingly and not – of the relations between their personal circumstances and the historic, economic, and class, ethnic, and racial relations and antagonisms within which they exist [Weis and Fine, 2013: 124-25].

Is Schola Coming Across as the Perfect Wife for Momany?

Marriage can be defined as a commitment and an ongoing exchange, involving more or less explicit contract that spells out the rights and obligations between partners (Beaujot, 1992: 286). I have discussed some of the ladies Momany lost as a possible spouse in the last chapter. While still talking about more of such lost cases in this and the next chapters, I will in this one mainly also talk about the woman he ended up marrying and who contrasts in some important ways with the wife he first lost. Very ambitious, humble, and grateful even for little things that you will not be expecting a "Thank you", Schola apparently came across as the perfect wife for Momany. She was very desirous of beginning her own family, having extremely clear ideas of how to bring up their children. Her devotion in this field fuelled many visits to 'medicine houses' when she seemed not to be "taking in" – her popular expression for being pregnant. In one of those 'medicine houses' in Douala, something strange happened; odd to Momany's companion, not to him. As soon as they had entered,

65

the 'medicine man' began shaking violently and staring at Momany as if very afraid. At last he said "Good thing you didn't go hunting. You have a strong star guiding you." And then turning to both of them he advised that nothing was wrong with the man and asking them to go well.

Schola was bewildered and asked what the meaning of all this was. Momany merely responded that he should rather be asking her the question since she was the one who had insisted in bringing him there, claiming that this particular 'medicine man' (as she had been told) was not as unreliable as those visited before him. Schola might not have understood what that 'medicine man' meant but her husband did; because it had to do with when Momany first got to Bamenda and lived in a home in Mile Two Nkwen where, "Finding the sand business thing not to be catching my attention, he [his host] began insisting that I go hunting with him in the night. I never obeyed my host's demands and left for my own place even as things were so hard on me, still believing strongly that money alone is not what is essential for success" (Fossungu, 2013a: 89).8 Momany did not then see the need to narrate all these things to Schola because she had proven not to be learning anything positive from most of the things from his past that he had told her; instead drawing only negative and naive conclusions from them. For example, she had placed the problem of not conceiving on her husband, suggesting that perhaps his sperms were insufficient to fertilize her. She was obviously naively drawing on his past with women that he had laid bare before her in the hope of aiding her know exactly who she has as husband. Could this openness trait in Momany also be behind his wife debacle? Imagine then what other conclusions that would have been drawn if Momany had stood firm on not visiting those

---

8 Ferguson (2008: 26 & 29-30) would even go further to argue that "Money is worth only what someone else is willing to give you for it" because "money is a matter of belief, even faith: belief in the person paying us, belief in the person issuing the money he uses or the institution that honours his cheques or transfers."

'medicine houses', or on (1) the use of letters for communication of certain issues and (2) staying away from the fertile virgin ground.

The Numerous Communications on Children

Schola's love for having children was strikingly impressive. During the four years they were apart (1995-99) she continued all through emphasizing on the children aspect (in her numerous communications to Momany) as the pressing reason why they needed to be together as soon as possible. For an exceedingly notable instance, on 13 March 1999 (just a month before she arrived in Canada) Schola wrote one of these letters to her husband stating in part:

My dear Power: ... I left the village only yesterday because of the sacrifices they asked me to make. Many things were done on me because it was discovered that some people are preventing us from succeeding in anything with witchcraft. I worked that one also. I would not want to write [all] what was said in the letter. I shall discuss with you when we are together. My stomach was also washed because they said those who are doing this to me are preventing me from having everything, even from giving birth. Anyway, everything was done and it was more serious this time.

More on letters and the africanscience being talked about in this particular letter will be exposed as we look at the woman's other characteristics, including her being fertile virgin ground for construction of necessary and desirable structures.

The Fertile Virgin Ground

This title certainly evokes uncertainty in the minds of some keen observers, especially in regard of the just alluded to infertility or problems of child-bearing. But read on. Unlike with Anna, Momany fell in love at first sight with Schola who also seems to be a kind of exceptional bridge to four of the ladies – Anna, Elizabeth, Christine, and Chantal (who is yet to be met) – that had prominently featured in his life as wife-material before her. Could this bridging trait have

67

anything to do with the first sight falling for her? Unlike Anna again Schola was not a virgin as such but looked like one, especially in her scope in several domains. This trait of hers clearly was virgin ground on which Momany thought he could easily design and construct the necessary and essential structures he wanted – an additional advantage to her very likeable character and physical beauty.

An example of what I am referring to as Schola's virginity in scope and the like could be picked up from her first letter to Momany in which she was talking about his earlier discussion with her in Fontem (South West Region) regarding her making her G.C.E. Advanced Level the academic year following. She had not passed it that August (a month after Momany had first met and fell for her) and he had told her to consider it "obtained now that I am part of your life." Her first note to him began with a mere "Hi". Of course, as you have seen and will continue to see, most of the girls start calling Momany darling (chéri), fiancé, Piero, and dear even at their first meeting; but here was Schola that Momany had not only just met but actually talked marriage to still addressing him weeks/months later with 'Hi'(and without his name at all). Can any other message(s) be picked up from that? Would you say Schola was really into this marital union 'with love and understanding' and, therefore, "for better and for worse"; or just in it because someone like a parent wants her to be in it? Put otherwise, was it an *ab initio* one-sided love and understanding relationship? Let's see what it could be, using these two broad heads (1) scholaparentism and onsilovundism and (2) the pregnancy story.

Scholaparentism and Onsilovundism (One-Sided Love and (Mis)Understanding)

The question of the role played by scholaparentism and onsilovundism on the failure of the Schola-Momany marriage certainly thrusts onto the table a discussion of the 'out-of-marriage' children; and the new definition of family in Canada, including the London divorce/child support suit – all of which incidents/excuses

68

seem to be just smokescreens for camouflaging scholaparentism (or callous parental greediness and ungratefulness). This is what some love and marriage experts would prefer to describe as inside versions of 99-Sensism. And what about the possibility of the involvement of africanscience in order to secure said scholaparentistic goals? I am not an ardent supporter of using africanscience to explain things but I do think that these are not issues to be taken lightly by anthropologists and other social scientists, including even the africanscientists themselves, who would want to really understand what Zembylos (2013: 19) describes as Schola's *"Den Xehno* [I don't forget]" attitude. To find out whether the entire marriage enterprise is an onsilovundistic (or a one-sided love and understanding) affair, I will be digging into two capital concerns, namely, (1) 'out of marriage' children, and (2) the re-conceptualization of family in Canada.

'Out of Marriage' Children

There appears to be some inverse and absorbing similarities between the Yoke Conspiracy from Anna's parents and Schola's Parental Spell. The latter that would be attempting to hide behind Momany's child saga, could show the way to not only one-sided love and (mis)understanding but also its corollary of putting dialogue over monologue. These out-of-marriage children are examined under two categories: children begotten before marriage and those during marriage.

Children Begotten Before Marriage

Momany had learnt about Kelie being his biological child while Schola was still in Cameroon. As complicated as the matter was (see Fossungu, 2013a: 159-161), he did not just write to Schola to tell her so and (as many would obviously have done) used it as pretext to ditch her. When he had brought Schola to Canada, he sat his wife down one day and explained to her, reasoning with her as follows. "You and I can actually choose who to have as a spouse; but a child never has that choice of who the parents are to be. Therefore, if Kelly is my daughter as I think she is (since viewing the whole messy

69

situation we are in, I do not think her mother would be joking about it), then I have to necessarily assume my responsibilities towards her as a father. This is what I must have to do, with you (my wife) only having the choice of deciding whether I do so *within* or *without* our marriage." Momany made it crystal-clear that whatever her decision on the marriage was, he was still going to help her become a Canadian permanent resident. At the time Schola chose to keep the marriage going. And it was apparently going well until she became a permanent resident of Canada in June 2000 while her husband was still on a one-entry student visa. Her attitude thereafter indicated to Momany that, by being frank (loving and understanding) in discussing the matter with her, he had spelt the end of the marriage. No problem about that at all since it was clearly an option he foresaw as being part of the love and understanding solely driving his frankness.

But Schola *et al* apparently had made up their minds for her not to go right away but only after five years when she must have first put Momany into a cavernous hole, as some sort of punishment for being truthful about his child? Is it not extremely difficult to deal with people whose whole life is based on scheming; people who never keep their word? People like this would be validating "Lorenzol himself [who] had put it in a song he composed in the 1470s: 'If you would be happy, be so. / There is no certainty about tomorrow'" (Ferguson, 2008: 47). It is hard to see how the Kelie-truthfulness could be the problem if Schola is actually the one who had made up her own mind to marry Momany, for better and for worse. Because she was not bold and truthful *ab initio* (see Fossungu, 2013a: 151-152), it is not very surprising that Schola has very undoubtedly shown herself to be incapable of handling the truth, becoming exceptionally bitter like Anna after the Yoke Conspiracy. Because of her unending desire to also render Momany acidic, Schola appears to have missed chances to look beyond Momany's errors (that are common to humankind) and to see the bitter-free man that married her. In short, she seems to have woefully failed to love and understand a man that loves and understands her like no other man would ever do. She and

70

her directors have thus also occupied themselves too much with trying to present Momany as a demon to people generally. But, as Momany has put it, all that cannot change him from what he knows he is and therefore cannot provide any reason for him to be bitter.

I have talked above about Schola's supplementary advantage (virginity in scope) to her likeable character and physical beauty. Her "added advantage" is obviously a two-sided sword in the sense that it also quickly and easily becomes fertile ground for her parents 'to design and construct their own necessary and essential structures' against the husband's, the more especially in the latter's long four-year absence. It is because Momany understands these things so well, in addition, that he can scarcely be bitter (above all not with the woman he has so dearly loved, and perhaps still loves?, and who is mother of their two wonderful children). All this holds because he can handle the bitter truth that his earnest desire to ameliorate people's life is part and parcel of the problem created for and through Schola. He is certainly part of the problem largely because of the type of person he is – someone who is not afraid of the truth and devotedly keeps his word: with or without the Kelie issue that has been used by Schola to explain or justify her Canadian monster-like behaviour.

But did all this happen solely because Momany was truthful about his daughter? No. Momany then thought he was actually breaking the news to Schola but subsequent events have shown that she and her parents knew about it (perhaps even before Momany did) long before she arrived in Canada. The fact that they knew about it before Schola ever landed in Canada already begs the question; but I will still analyze it from the assumption that she only knew about it from her husband as noted above, because it still does not tie in nor justify her new re-conceptualization of family; nor tally in with mutual love and understanding. Rita, as you have seen in Chapter 1, loved Momany in school but her love appeared to have increased ten-fold when he was truthful to her about the side of him at home that she could never have known but for his telling her. Their love thus grew from strength to strength despite that an essential part of the relationship

71

(routine sex) was 'painfully' missing. Yet, many who knew them then would hardly believe today reading that they were not then regularly "doing bad thing". Real or pure love is not just about sex; lust is. Christickinology has also made that point exceedingly understandable. Love, they say, can change anything, everything. That is what love and understanding would be all about.

Now, not to be seen as absolving Momany from some blame in the matter, is Schola's behaviour regarding Momany's being upfront with her regarding his daughter (conceived before his marriage to her) not pure evidence that she is a patient of nonoselfism, that is, that she does not know herself or what she is up against? Or that the Kelie issue is just being used as a 'cover' or smokescreen for the real 99-sensical and/or africanscientific issues of scholaparentism? These questions are very important to ask for a number of reasons. First, you would easily comprehend what is being said here if you know the kind of ideal woman Schola was from when Momany met and married her until he left Cameroon. For a simple example, Momany's friend, Solomon, and his family took care of the honeymoon by inviting the bride and groom to their residence in Yaoundé. It was simply beyond description what this couple did for the newly married duo; but I can only stress that they had brought other important Momany friends (both female and male) from far and wide to the occasion in order for them "to see this very lucky woman" called Schola. Momany thereafter happily took Schola to other cities in the South West Region where he had lived and the numerous receptions were not different; not to even mention the stream of letters and other gifts from his across-Atlantic friends in Edmonton. Schola was so impressed by the attention and respect and admiration she was receiving.

She even later told her husband the following (while they were in Buea to secure her an apartment and a place in Lycée Musolé where she was to prepare for her G.C.E. Advanced Level): "Power, thank you for making me the happiest woman on earth. I promise to do all my best to see that you too are forever the happiest man on the planet." And, frankly, Momany has emphasized, that was precisely

72

what Schola had been doing and doing so well too like Anna until Momany triumphantly left for Canada in search of the best for all of them; and truly feeling armed (in Anna's incomparable words) "with my love wrapped around you as it is [that] there is nothing you cannot successfully do." Schola then arrived in Montréal in April 1999 through her *Power*'s indefatigable efforts; apparently having completely effaced or left her very short memory for good deeds behind in a dirty rubbish bin, bringing along only the very long *Den Xehno* one for ugly deeds. Why? This one-word question could also lead you straight to the question of what it really was that had delayed Schola that she "left the village only yesterday because of the sacrifices *they* [who?] asked me to make. Many things were done on me...." (Schola's letter of 13 March 1999, cited above) She promised in that same letter to discuss these "things" with Momany when they would be together but that has never happened since she got to Canada. To pose the question again, what could be some of these "many things" that "were done" on/to the ideal wife that Momany once knew and had that completely transformed her to the fiend you are now reading about? If the hideous comportment is indeed because of children begotten before marriage to her, then what is one to make of children begotten during marriage?

Children Begotten During Marriage

The querying is very significant in the sense that Schola's own father has had a child (during marriage to her mother) with their neighbour and this child (Schola's half-sister) is being brought up together with them by Schola's mother. Could Schola have truly learnt nothing from that? Could sibling togetherness and stability be some of the overriding concerns of Schola's mother? I cannot exactly tell but the attitude of Schola (who seems to be so much under the parents' remote cross-continental africanscientific direction) seems to give an affirmative to this question because Schola has never failed to spot an occasion to lavishly talk to Momany about her siblings from far and wide (Sweden, Norway, Belgium, Denmark, Montreal, Calgary, you name them) converging, for example, in Michigan, USA, with her for a *family reunion*. This only goes to reinforce her new and awkward definition of family (without children and spouse).

This ranting is likely intended to produce sullenness in Momany, but here is the bitter 'love and understanding' truth that instead ensues: If *family reunion* with other siblings is really the important thing in the uncalled for ranting, why then do Schola and her mother not also see the need for the two children Momany has with her to, once in a while, also reunite with their other siblings (and father)? Half or full, they are brothers and sisters and nobody can change that fact. Once more, I must have to repeatedly ask, if sibling reunion is so important to Schola (as it also seems to be to her mother), why don't they also see the need for the two children Momany has with her also regularly reuniting with the others he has with the other two women? As they don't also see the need for keeping some of these issues 'within the house', is there any reason why it shouldn't be publicly talked about now? Being her son-in-law, Momany denies ever even hearing or knowing most of these things from Schola's mother; only being aware of this particular half-sister case when Schola herself had been talking about it on the phone with her numerous friends in the United States, Britain, and elsewhere at the same time as she was broadcasting the Kelie issue.

This comportment makes one wonder if there is something much larger that Momany is unaware of; because if it is indeed the Kelie issue that actually belies the blinkeredness of the wife he once knew as the ideal, then one can try to figure this other mutual love and understanding issue out for Schola in particular. Momany had given her his word in November 1993, "for better and for worse". But while he is in Canada, with her still in Cameroon (with not even a child tying them together), Momany learnt of Kelie. Instead of acting the way he did – a person who means and keeps his/her word – he immediately used that as excuse to dump her. In this scenario, would this word-keeper be right in claiming to have had any iota of love for and understanding of her? I am sure there would be general accord here that only a liar like Schola would answer *yes* here; and strongly

74

attesting are both her re-conceptualization of the meaning of family and her playing around with pregnancy and children while in Canada.

Re-Conceptualizing the Meaning of Family 99-Sensically

Momany appears to have learnt more about Schola than she could ever learn about him or even about herself; this perhaps also being indicative of their respective degrees of interest in and commitment to the marriage relationship. This thesis may explain a lot of what has happened to a relationship that was evidently the envy of many of their associates. Talking of the possibility of africanscience involvement, Momany has interestingly postulated that "I have often told my wife (who refuses to learn, which is normal when you are so short-ranged; or have been so intoxicated with what, I still doesn't know), that wise people sometimes play the idiot mostly because they know it is in that position that they can actually appreciate just how far others would go considering them to be silly." He believes that Schola's refusal to learn that life is not all about take and take and take (just because the giver is giving without fighting back) has affected and still will heavily impact on the future of their children. These children, Momany hopes, should be able to know that they may be growing up with just one parent principally because the absent parent loves them so much, just as he did/does to their mother.

Just imagine this again. While most of the ladies (virgins for that matter) have been falling for Momany at first sight and professing same, it was him who instead fell in love with Schola at first sight. And (even more extraordinary) he did not even first "go out with her" before asking her hand in marriage. It is kind of strange for this strange 'virgins' man' called Momany, isn't it? Was it an error? However one looks at it, the familiar fact is that Momany is a man who does not get into doing anything unless he wants to do it right and to the best of his ability (Fossungu, 2013a: 133). Momany has since marrying Schola never had a second thought or ulterior motive while doing anything to or for her. His basic goal has been to advance their basic family (Schola, their children and himself) and, by African extension, parents, brothers and sisters from both sides, and over. As a bigger picture person, he sees the task of "helping the greatest number of persons possible" being more easily accomplished by both of them working together than working alone. He therefore did all any serious and committed husband or wife would do to get her out of Cameroon and into Canada. Always with the financial help of his white friends, Andrew and Nancy (of Edmonton), he did put her into the Canadian system without himself first being inside. Is this not very unlike most scheming people, especially from the part of the world they come from, would normally do? Is that not precisely what love, dedication and marriage/family should entail: provided it is not endlessly one-sided (or conniving) but reciprocal?

Warning! If you have never encountered insularity and its handmaid of ungratefulness, then you are with all of them right now! This is exactly what the specialists on the Science of Cameroonian Ethnic Epithetization would rather be calling the 99-Sensism of never selling a hen for fear it would produce chicken for buyers and thus prevent them from endlessly purchasing from the 99-senser. You are now deeply inside the 99-Sensism Love-and-Marriage Marketplace. Schola's refugee claim in Canada is based on her harassment in Cameroon consequent on the critical writings of her husband (Momany). Yet, when (through that husband's tireless efforts) Canada offers her refuge, he is no longer part of her signification of family, not to even talk about his own safety. Don't start wondering as yet; there is more. After having settled his wife's immigration expenses (with loans still from Andrew and Nancy), Momany recalls how he used to struggle all alone to foot the other bills (phone, hydro, internet, etc), pay rents, put food on the table, and generally look after the children while Schola was busy studying in Concordia University (2001-2002) and McGill University (2002-2004). Unlike the foreign student that he was, as a permanent resident and studying, Schola was entitled to all sorts of bursaries and student loans which never came into the picture at home even when at times meeting up with monthly rents (then 700.00$) was so

76

difficult that Momany had to stretch his hands left and right to get loans (with extremely high interests) from just anyone in order that they could continue having a roof over them. Indeed, even when her husband's one-year work permit expired in October 2001 before the renewal could arrive and he could not work without it for more than two months, Schola did not step in to help but instead created nasty scenes when anything was lacking at home.[9]

---

[9] You clearly get some of these nasty situations from the response or rectification of the Respondent (Momany) to the fake nature of the Applicant's (Schola's) divorce claim, where she stated that "We separated in August 2003. Before this separation he moved out and came back a couple of times. For example, he moved out in September 2002 when I was pregnant with my son. He returned when the baby was about to be born." Court File N° F1162/05 (Superior Court of Justice, Family Court, London, Ontario, 2006). And said response from Momany was:

Doesn't this, standing on its own as it is, make anybody without the full facts make a real monster of me? Why are the exact circumstances surrounding these various "moving outs" not even mentioned? Let us take the September 2002 example she cites. What else would any reasonable person in my position have done to avoid being put behind bars? You are sitting right there and your pregnant wife is on the phone talking to someone else about you in terms that the person on the other end (if told) would not believe that you are there also hearing all what s/he is hearing. You hold yourself together as much as you have grown used to but the provocation mounts to a point where you realize you are about to lose your cool and you then quietly leave the scene. Later you come back home and, while you are trying to take a nap on the sofa, you feel your pregnant wife's grip on your throat, nagging all this time because you left the scene of her provocation without exactly giving her the much-searched reason for having you arrested. If you succeed in non-violently freeing yourself from this choking enterprise (as I did), what would you do to eschew a worse scenario? Yes, I moved out a couple of times always to avoid a worse situation from developing. To say, in this particular example, that I moved in only when our son was about to be born (his birth date is 1 April 2003), is to ignore important facts and create confusion. Has the Applicant forgotten that I had moved [back] in before going to Cameroon on 18 October 2002 for the burial of my father who passed away on 11 October 2002? And I did not spend more than a month in Cameroon. Does the Applicant also forget that when she left with the children to London, Ontario, in September 2004 they actually left me in the same house or address and in a financial catastrophe? [*Id*: "Putting the Facts Straight", pp. 2-3.]

77

Wouldn't anyone venture, like me, to think that in life one must try not to always be at the receiving end? Otherwise, is one ever to know what it is like to be at the other end? Would such a person's then 'accidentally' being one day anywhere near the other end not be a sure fatality? For an appetizer or tip of the iceberg to this 'other-end' theory, just hear Schola's funny claim for child support in the London court in 2006 to begin comprehending the thinking of the take and take and take people: "Currently, I am struggling in raising these children financially and will like him to support me...." [Court File N° F1162/05 (Superior Court of Justice, Family Court, London, Ontario, 2006)] To begin with, is raising children only a *financial* issue? Let's stay however with the financial that is all Schola obviously always sees. She (with a professional or "good" job) is struggling like no one has ever done in raising just two children *financially* but she obviously did not see just how Momany (with an "odd job") had been doing *same* to two adults plus the same two children and was only getting all the shit he was getting from her. Theory validated or falsified? Let us this far leave court issues and examples and get squarely back to the immigration matters we are on. Since Momany had met and married her in 1993, for the very first time he needed a little "push" from Schola in 2000 in the form of her sponsoring him as her spouse (with him footing the bills, of course) so that he could also become a Canadian permanent resident before graduating from Université de Montréal in December 2000. As a permanent resident just finishing school in Canada one has all the chances of getting straight into the professions (Schola's case being typical). No such chances exist for someone on a mere foreign student visa. Most professional jobs that Momany could be considered for are directed only to Canadian permanent residents and citizens. Despite explaining all these things to her, Schola's response to Momany was: "I cannot sponsor you because (1) I know the day you will get papers you will run and (2) I must go to school in order to have a good job so as to be able to help my brothers, sisters, and parents" [numbering supplied].

78

Mutual love and understanding or mulovundism indeed, you would say this is? Are obtrusive cases like this one not what would lead some to the conclusion that Bangwa are 99-sensers that do not sell hens but only cocks? Was this not what the parents of Momany's two virgin spouses-to-be (who might surely have given and shared with him two-sided love and understanding) were so afraid of in Momany who does not even seem to exhibit that 'general' Bangwa trait? Like in the case of the dominant male in marital unions, therefore, one should be wary of some of these generalizations.[10] But then, are general rules not often (if not always) derived from observed particular cases? In other words (as Cameroon's *lingua franca* or Kamtok would spice it up), *No bi na one wow-wow coco di spoil fufu?* Indeed, this other practical Inside Arm of 99-Sensism appears to have largely spoiled Momany's once-thought delicious *fufu and eru* (for more on this and other 'popular national' Cameroonian dishes, see Anyefru, 2013). As Momany has firmly indicated, he has never felt more insulted in his whole life than when he got that from someone he then called wife and who, moreover, would never be where she is but for him. It was a gratuitous insult that, Momany says, is responsible, directly and indirectly, for a holder of so many academic credentials, including a doctorate degree in law, working in the forest. Not that doing that job is the worst thing he has ever done as job in his life; adding that "I always try to successfully make positives out of what others would consider to be negatives." Whatever Momany wants to make of it, I will prefer to instead talk a little about the implications of Schola's response, beginning with the second arm.

Good Job and the Aiding of Siblings and Parents

The bitter truth here is that things would have been different and better (not just for Momany and their children) if his wife had

---

[10] There is a strong tendency for people to generalize from a group to an individual, which is one likely source of prejudice and stereotyping. Things that are true on the average, however, are not always true in particular cases (Reaves, 1992: 28).

sponsored him to become a permanent resident. He would then have been landed in Canada before, or not very long after, graduating in December 2000. If you know the stupid and roundabout Canadian immigration regulations in this regard well enough (see Fossungu, 2013a: 144 n.15), you will easily understand the rest of the story. Schola insinuates in this second arm of her response, first, that Momany had been doing all sorts of "odd jobs" to maintain and educate her (from, and including, her G.C.E. Advanced Level to Master of Social Work) in particular because he did not go to school; and, secondly, that he had been concentrating all efforts on her as his wife because he did not have brothers, sisters, and parents. Could that be true?

Contrary to what Schola presents to them, Momany would appear to have nothing against the fact that she has been helping her siblings and parents. He sees it all as still being part of the attainment of his objectives, done indirectly or directly, with these siblings and parents of hers being encapsulated in the "greatest number of persons possible" that he wants to ameliorate things for. Those people, for instance, that Sam stopped bullying because of his mother's creative use of Momany's Mr. English reputation (see Fossungu, 2013a: 39-42), are also caught in "the greatest number possible" net. Also, those who are getting the benefits of 'soft landing' through the CGAM or Cameroon Goodwill Association of Montreal are also captured, whether or not Momany personally knows them (Fossungu, *id*: 122-132). It does not necessarily have to be himself aiming the direct blows at their woes. This is clearly in line with what Momany's father said in regard of his tenant, Mr. Lucas (*id*: 8-9). Momany is very glad then that, unlike Flavie (as you will see later in Flaviqueenism – chapter 4), Schola has at least expanded "the greatest number of persons possible".

What Momany does not quite understand however is why Schola makes the two processes (sponsoring him and helping her parents/siblings) incompatible: except she means in effect that Momany must forever remain in her *financial* prison (footing all the bills then, and now re-named to child support) in order to insure her

80

being able to help those limited number of people (without Momany also being able to help anyone else, including his own children). That is so blinkered and even goes further than just "burn[ing] the bridge after you have crossed it" (Fossungu, 2013a: 106) to also effectively eliminating the bridge-builder so that no other bridge could ever be erected. Much corroboration to this particular 99-sensically scholaparentistic thesis is derived from the other arm regarding Momany's getting papers and running.

Getting Papers and Running

Despite the affront that, alone, was enough to provoke the "running", Momany was still there for Schola and the kids (and her siblings and parents), putting his solid desire to make things better for the greatest number of persons possible before his "personal career". Now, to those talking bitterness in the man called Momany, I would say this: Just show me that bitter person that would not only still be around the person that is causing his/her bitterness but also be actively helping that person: and I would have shown you a bitter-free person. Because we are here talking "scheming" and "running", it must be further noted that in 2001 and 2002, successively, Momany had been appointed Yale University`s Civic Education Project (CEP) Visiting Lecturer to the University of Moscow (Russian Federation) and the University of Minsk (Belarus), respectively. In regard of the 2001 recruitment, it could be idiotically argued that he did not yet "have Canadian papers" and that is why he did not "run". I say foolishly because Momany did not even need those "Canadian papers" to get out of Canada. But if the argument is based on re-entry, what about 2002 when Momany already "had Canadian papers"? He became a Canadian permanent resident in March 2002 without passing through Schola and was still there for her and her "family".

Is Momany's comportment not what could be clearly characterized as one-sided love and understanding? And should one also go ahead and say this onsilovundism is a veritable crucible for failure? In other words, does one-sided love and understanding not also beget success in a sense? Wouldn't only birds 'not always flocking with birds of the same feather' be able to see this? It is needless describing here Schola's surprise-and-wonder when she learnt (through opening his "Personal and Confidential" letters – the unmistakeable deeds of schemers and backstabbers?) that Momany had become a permanent resident despite her having closed what she narrow-mindedly saw as the only door for him into Canada. How small minds stay small all the time! Having gone this far through Momany's unique tale, I wonder if the reader is also wondering a lot if Schola has herself ever for one minute contemplated on what would have become of her and all her brothers, sisters and parents if Momany had "run" to, or left for, Eastern Europe then in hot pursuit of his own professional development. Don't you think that is precisely what he must have done if he were as short-sighted or narrow-minded and scheming as the person talking about his running? Who even actually ran and why?

Schola chose the London job over the same opportunity in Montréal because (as she incessantly put it to her friends) "He [Momany] will be a parasite on me if I take the job in Montreal." Who should normally be talking "parasitic" here? If Momany was not the loving and understanding type but actually the "parasitic" and "running" type, would he have even waited to bring Schola into Canada before running and being 'parasitic'? A very simple response, it is indeed. It is only normal, of course, that if you are not planning to run/parasite, the running/parasitic idea will never be part of your vocabulary or dictionary. In the same way, only backstabbers always think everyone else is planning to backstab them. They thus live in perpetual fear and are consequently unable to see the bigger picture of things that usually would permit the open-minded to advance in spite of the roadblocks, such as a divorce suit that is nothing other than an attempt to prevent others from also benefitting from the existence of the elastic and unbreakable bridge called Momany. To say therefore that children have now become mere commodities for acquiring wealth would not be to stretch the point, an argument that is reinforced by Schola's own share in the Pregnancy Story.

The Pregnancy Story

Someone once said they overheard Momany's father telling a friend of his that he was very proud of Momany, especially as he seems to know exactly what he was doing or wants to do; specifically saying: "Look at the number of girls I have had to see he was dating; yet I have not been inundated with a series of unwanted pregnancies." In a way Momany's father was right; in another, so wrong in the sense of again being right. As this statement would somewhat be confusing to those of you not "greatly assisted by the teachings of the Palm Wine School of Deconstruction" (Fossungu, 2013c: 11), I must have to explain it further. The fact that Momany has had his fair share of pregnancy woes and revelations makes his father wrong but right since the father has never been inundated with them, the result of Momany knowing exactly what he was doing – thanks to his always looking at the larger picture. The pregnancy story is a complex, long, revealing, and obstructing one in Momany life. The ones he authors do date back as far as Manjo. It is thus not new or restricted to Canada. The non-Momany and revealing ones predate Manjo. The entire pregnancy tale would involve (1) those like his wife's playing around with pregnancy and children, including the rebellious girl and the Yaoundé bone-digging virgin; followed by (2) virtuous ignorance and revealing pregnancy.

Scholizyvettism or the Playing Around with Children and Pregnancy

As the title here shows, scholizyvettism is the act of selfishly jockeying around with children (pregnancy and abortion). This scholizyvettical side of the pregnancy story looks at the 99-sensical and trapping use of pregnancy and children and has two arms: Schola's trapping use of pregnancy and children in Canada and the rebellious girl's and the Yaoundé bone-digging virgin's entrapment/coercion roles of pregnancy in Cameroon.

The Canadian Pregnancy Trapper

While still in Cameroon, you have seen that Schola's love of having children drove the couple into several juju houses in the country. But already in Canada and a Canadian permanent resident; and having also secured admission into McGill University that would secure a good job for her with which to help her siblings and parents (the only components of her re-definition of family), Cameroon's child-loving Schola can afford to single-handedly go about terminating a four-month pregnancy on 7 March 2002 (Black Thursday) at the Royal Victoria Hospital in Montréal. That was their second child. It devastated Momany as well as their little girl who was then two. Isn't that quite baffling? But that is not all. Schola also used pregnancy for their son (normally their third child) only as a trap to ensure the wellbeing of those she considers her family (siblings and parents). After her 2002 abortion, Momany left Montréal for Edmonton for some fresh air and environment. He had not been there for a week when Schola lied about their daughter being so sick, knowing of course how attached their daughter and Momany were. When he returned to Montréal, against Nancy's womanly advice that it was a ploy, Schola then got pregnant. Momany did not see that pregnancy as a problem though because the main reason for her being in Canada (quite apart from her claim of harassment in Cameroon because of Momany's thinking) was for the family to grow while they were both progressing academically and professionally.

Nancy was quite right and Momany kind of knew it. But he explains that he was not going to punish his child because of the mother's scheming. Momany is apparently someone who always looks ahead; which is why a lot of people usually fail to see what he sees, leading to the infamous "four eyes" description. He well understood that all Schola wanted was for him to be around footing the bills as usual while she spends every dime that came into her hands on her parents, brothers, and sisters. This agenda is of such capital importance to her that there is simply a zero tolerance toward anything that even thinly stands in the way (the four-month abortion pointedly testifying) and who knows what would have become of the

84

children if she did not get what they were being employed to obtain? Paradoxically, Canada's anti-children Schola has since September 2004 been working with a children aid society. That was Canada and its callous abortion and pregnancy's obstructing role and the 99-sensical definition of family. But pregnancy's 99-sensical road-blocking role began in Manjo with the rebellious girl.

Cameroon's Pregnancy Users: The Rebellious Girl and Yaoundé Bone-Digging Virgin

Momany's pregnancy woes not beginning until Manjo would seem to be the handiwork of the AAD. The Annastasian Automatic Door must have greatly aided Momany in avoiding "adventures" with most of the attention-seeking girls who are most often at the base of unwanted or rushed-unto pregnancies. The fact that Manjo was the watershed of the issue is largely attributed to a parent's stroppy and domineering attitude towards her daughter that led to rebellion and the unthinking consequences in her bitter response – **The Rebellious Girl**. Thus, about a month after Momany's visit to the home of Elizabeth's parents in Kumba, he had to grapple hard with the question as to whether he was then ready to lead Elizabeth on to marriage, with or without the consent of her parents, mother especially. I am here talking about when Elizabeth had broken the news of her pregnancy to Momany, a thing that she said happened that same evening she had rebelled against her mum. As Momany puts it, "As my clock-ticking head did not explode then, it will never do so. Much as I loved her and wanted to be a father, I still had to keep my personal preference out (the Ritaian crisebacology being very serviceable again) and look at the bigger picture in regard of all three parties – child, mother, and father."

In fairness to Elizabeth (and to Anna that she was immediately replacing), some people would rush to postulate that love is blind. But is love really that blind to realities or understanding? Could it not be the question of one's bitter emotions ruling reason rather the other way round? It seems as if (rebellious) Elizabeth wanted to use this pregnancy solely to become Momany's wife against her mother's stance; a decision that she had hastily taken without considering the consequences on both the child and Momany, and even herself. For example, what kind of relationship was to exist between this Bangwa child and its anti-Bangwa grandma, especially when Momany was not to be there? (Just look at what must have happened to an ideal adult spouse in the person of Schola in Momany's four-year absence!) Yes, he was not going to be there not because Momany chose not to be; it was in prison that he was to be, either way (officially and familial-wise). That is exactly what the position at the time was for a teacher impregnating his student, the gravity augmenting especially in small towns like Manjo. Imprisonment could then be avoided only by private marital arrangement with the parents who would then withdraw their child from school before the 'witch-hunting' school authorities became aware of the pregnancy and especially its author. Could this option have conveniently happened, knowing where Elizabeth's mum stood on the matter of her daughter marrying a Bangwa? What about her schooling and Momany's? Isn't it clear that Elizabeth wouldn't have rushed into this but for her mother's uncompromising posture?

Indeed, some parents are still clearly oblivious of the fact that their children are born in an era that is very different from theirs. For instance, some time ago, a man with many wives (mostly, if not completely, chosen by his own parents) had little or no problems governing his *foyer*. Not exactly so today with just two or three wives that he has himself selected, thus presenting, for example, this familiar situation where "Things only went from bad to worse in Uncle Ngufor's home, turning this fine gentleman into a heavy drinker and what have you" (Fossungu, 2013a: 157). Elizabeth's mother's Bangwaphobia and the fact that her daughter fell 'madly' in love with a Bangwa called Momany, would be so overwhelming that even her daughter's mother-chosen husband (who has never even met Momany) knows so much about the wife's 'Bangwa sweetheart'. Question for the experts: Has this mother ever been considering anyone else outside herself when she behaves as such?

The consequences of and fallouts from this mother's egocentric comportment have really mounted to the point where the said man too would *moutonly* go straight on and heartlessly terminate his wife's four-to-five-month pregnancy (his very own child): just on learning that Momany was briefly in Cameroon! I would not want to drag the matter on but I am sure you can already clearly see what the hell children (including Momany from a 99-sense household) are/have been going through simply because of 99-Sensism. Elizabeth was surely and largely speaking for the numerous anguishing children when she agonizingly wept on the phone to Momany in 2007: "Fiancé, I just cannot come to terms with the fact that I have had to needlessly lose two beloved children – one from you (my first love) and my first child ever, who would have been thirty-four now, and the other from my own husband – all simply because of my own mother's baseless anti-Bangwa disposition. What also doubly aggravates my pain is the fact that I did not even have sexual intercourse with you while you were briefly here and almost got killed by thieves. But my husband has killed his own child, claiming it was yours!" What rubbish that is emanating from a mother and grand-mother! I am sure Elizabeth was in so much anguish that she added ten more years to the age of her "first child ever", judging from when the conception took place. But let's hear the Manjo pregnancy tale regarding "my first child ever" to the end.

On the side of the school authorities, it was simply suicidal for them to have the least idea; especially because of the principal's hostile or venom-like attitude towards Momany, as well as toward Elizabeth that the principal had been trying to date over the years, to no avail. He had once called Momany to his office and threatened to expose him for having fake certificates, a story obviously tied to another inside version of 99-Sensism, in the nature of Mr. Bangwa-man versus Momany's "going-to-Yaoundé" strategy (see Fossungu, 2013a: 119-122). Momany had very uninterestedly told the principal to go to any hell where his diplomas would be certified for counterfeit. Imagine the principal now really having substance on which to stand against both of his 'enemies'! That must never happen and Momany had to act as fast and carefully as possible.

Like he had done with Rita in SHS Fiango in Kumba with bolargumentalism, Momany therefore sat Elizabeth down and reasoned with her in the most cordial and loving manner he could, laying bare in front of her all the consequences she had not considered in her swift move to get pregnant. She understood and welcomed the abortion option; Momany also understanding perfectly then that the issue was her way of getting him hooked on marriage when she added: "I hope you won't abandon me after this is over." He simply said it was pressing they resolve the problem at hand first and worry about what happens thereafter after. They headed together for the hospital in the nearby city of Nkongsamba the next day and were given a date and conditions for the abortion. To Momany, it was a very devastating thing to do, it not being even easy just coming up with the payment; expenses that occasioned Momany's impromptu trip to Nwangong, where he got a peculiar 100%-royal love and marriage transforming experience with his cousin, better known as *cousilovism.*

Cousilovism: Reaching the village from Manjo, Momany was heavily mesmerized by this girl of about six (same age he himself first fell in love?) who threw him into a marriage trance. How can this fellow have fallen so deeply in love (as a child) with an adult (mandenguelovism) and then (as an adult himself) also fallen in same manner and degree with a child (cousilovism)? What could the causal link be, if any? In a kind of reverie the little was being happily married to Momany right there in Letia quarter. At that time he was sort of vacillating and leaning towards never marrying due to the Anna love-attack in Yoke, fortified by the Manjo pregnancy crisis that even unexpectedly brought him to the village. This Nwangong Love-and-Marriage Incident was kind of very strange but also sweetly transforming for Momany as it had instantly and magically changed or settled his mind on the subject of marriage.

When he got to the palace where Mami Regina (his birth mother) was then living, he very excitedly told his birth mother that he had found his wife in Letia and would show her that wife-to-be before leaving so that his mother could keep an eye on the girl as she grew up. Momany was now fully back into marriage, almost forgetting the problems that had then brought him to Nwangong. Mami Regina too was excited at the news; but Momany later on found out that the wife-to-be in question was his cousin and left the village without bringing the matter up again; but many troubling questions did remain on his mind. Very unlike other mothers in her place and time, his birth mother has never (until now) asked a question about the girl Momany had excitedly promised showing to her. Neither has she ever pressed him to marry. What kind of mother is Momany's biological mother? Does she (as well as Momany's young cousin) actually communicate with him without saying a thing? Most importantly, why did Momany 'chicken out' from making tradition by breaking tradition through marrying his cousin with whom he so desperately fell in love? This is not a new question and Fossungu (2013a: 163-65) has attempted some explanations that are worth filling in here.

Fossungu obviously has argued the points brilliantly but it would appear that those arguments do not explain why Momany did prefer to deny his natural inclinations towards love and understanding and to divert to something else just because of some (outmoded?) traditional barrier. Most graphically, why was Momany not as bold and truthful then, and could his marriage messes so far be his cousin's unique magical way of bringing him "home to me" (to borrow from the magic of Christine who, interestingly, had immediately *temporarily* filled the cousin's prohibited place in his heart)? Could this fact or connection in any way also explicate the eerie gaffe with Christine? Is Momany the weird person in the whole matrix? How come this little girl (his cousin) could have affected him mandenguelovistically when at that very time he was less interested in the many mature girls in Manjo who were flinging themselves at him and very ready for marriage, including even using pregnancy to get him hooked up?

Whatever the answers to the Nwangong Strange Cousilovistic Marriage may be, Momany was glad everything thereafter went well in Manjo, without any complications afterwards with Elizabeth. He had vowed then this was not a decision he ever wanted to make again; coming to the realization (like was the case with Charlotte during the Genesis-to-Sasse *Charalicism*) that, much as he loved her, continuing with Elizabeth presented obvious risks not only to his keeping that promise but also to his then UNIYAO bid. That there was much love between Elizabeth and Momany, there is no doubt. But that there also would be understanding is not clear. For instance, why did they have to get to this pregnancy point in the first place? In other terms, why did Momany not discuss his plans for UNIYAO with Elizabeth as he had done with Anna? Why did Elizabeth not discuss pregnancy with Momany if it needed to be used by both of them as a tool to surmount her mom's stance against their envisaged marriage? What contribution to this apparent lack of communication or understanding comes from their teacher-student relationship?

From my reading of the facts, what would seem to have really irritated Momany could not be Elizabeth's getting pregnant to secure her place as his wife; but two things that do not tie in were particularly noted, quite apart from her mother's awkward position. First, she came heavily accompanied by someone (a "sister") when she broke the news to Momany; later explaining to him it was because she was afraid of him (whereas she was never afraid of him, as a total stranger to her, on that first day?). Furthermore, Momany clearly did not see himself with a wife that would be afraid to talk about any issue with him, one-on-one. You have seen the catastrophe that this kind of love-and-fear relationship engenders, when Anna's mother (apparently desirous of what is good for Anna) could not weigh in regarding her daughter's future because of her fear of her husband. Another thing could be Elizabeth's getting pregnant without Momany's knowledge and consent; a comportment that could in a way be juxtaposed with Schola's egocentric gambling with children and/or pregnancy. The main point being made is that both (prospective) parents have to dialogue on the matter of children without one party unilaterally using pregnancy and/or abortion as mere tool(s) for acquiring some advantages. For instance, if I talk below in chapter 4 about Momany not having a post-flop backup plan for Anna, that will be as far as he alone was concerned because, as a pair, they secretly had pregnancy as their backup to anyone trying to tear them apart (could Anna have unwittingly and naively divulged the plan to her mother?). This plan was not used only because of the masterful scheming that put a wide gulf between them before the fatal separation – thanks principally to Anna's love for letters or monologue over one-on-one dialogue.

The Yaoundé Bone-digging Virgin: Talking of dialogue also brings to this pregnancy narrative a Bamileke lady called Yvette; with her pregnancy fairy-tale being almost the reverse to that of Elizabeth (also Bamileke) but very identical to Schola's 99-sensical one. Highly gifted, calmly passionate, innately beautiful, and with a smile that digs right into Momany's bones, Yvette is a virgin that he met in a high school in Yaoundé in which he was teaching. He talked about marrying her and she was so excited and agreed. This is Yaoundé and at this time Momany is also in the doctoral programme and after all the curious messes in the spouse-domain in this city (detailed out in chapter 4), he thought all that mystery had just been leading him to Yvette. The Elizabeth-type of obstacles are no longer there, especially as Momany had known quite a lot from Yvette about her open-minded parents and siblings that he was yet to meet or see. Things were moving so well between them and Yvette and Momany decided to have a baby, with the understanding of formalizing everything before the baby's arrival.

About a week after she "missed her period", Yvette greatly surprised Momany not only with talk of her 'discovering' she was pregnant but also that her senior sister (that Momany never met) already had a doctor for the abortion for which he needed to pay by handing the stated amount to her, Yvette. Well, it was very hard on Momany who was very concerned with the promise he had made in Manjo on abortions, the more so as this pregnancy was supposedly mutually planned. It was thus not because of the large amount of

91

money demanded but Momany just wanted to have a one-on-one dialogue again with Yvette on the issue; so he suggested her coming home so they could go and see someone who could do the same thing at a much lower amount. This was just like unintentionally declaring war with Lucifer because hell then broke loose with all sorts of threats that her sister had enumerated in the event that Momany does not comply. It was truly hard for Momany to recognize the person he was listening to as the wonderful Yvette that he had known till then. He found it very unbelievable and really heartbreaking. She got the money eventually but that was the end of the relationship as far as Momany was concerned; explaining why all her subsequent diehard attempts to continue with it were fruitless. The specialists would want to find out if Yvette was actually pregnant or just feigning it? If she had later changed her mind about giving birth, what was so difficult in discussing that with Momany? Was she just being remote-controlled like Schola (scholaparentism) and Jane and Odilia (janodilism)? Was Yvette truthful about the sister's threats and did she actually know what she really wanted (nonoselfism)?

The foregoing scholizyvettists are very unlike Christine who is a total stranger to nonoselfism, quite apart from her very enlightening christickinology lessons. This woman knew exactly what she wanted and who she was. Even without Momany's conceding about it, I would venture to say Christine is the most truthful and respectfully bold of all the Momany women since Anna. "Even as I narrate this story to you," Momany could not help lamenting, "something so strong inside me keeps telling me that Christine is the woman I should have married at twenty-four or -five." To sustain his 'something so strong inside', Momany also pointed, inter alia, to the fact that he actually had a similar Yvette-like pregnancy dialogue with Christine in September 1984. The plan was to get her pregnant before Momany leaves for Yaoundé where she was to later join him. Describing Christine as Momany's "younger identical twin-sister" would be the best way, I think, of saying that both of them shared so much in perspectives and scope to the extent of seeming to share the same clock-ticking head. With Christine, Momany never had to do too much thinking before presenting any idea to her because she did a lot of thinking (or christickinologize) herself on whatever issue they had on the table. And this is where Christine was so very special to Momany; never just agreeing with him simply to avoid disagreement. Christine did not only reject his point but also was very clear on and extraordinarily convincing in her point: "Chéri, you know as much as I do that it is great joy for me to be both your wife and the mother of our children. But I do not want it to appear as if you are tied down to me just because I am carrying our child. Go my love, and when everything is in place, as you say, come and see my people and get me; I will always be waiting for you. Moreover, I think it is best for our children to come when we are both together and ready for them, what do you think?"

Momany did not say a thing for quite some time, just staring at this young wisdom and highly wondering if leaving for Yaoundé without Christine was worth it. He then knew so many women that would talk to the father of the baby they are carrying, referring to the baby as "your child", never "our child" as Christine did. Even his wife uses her most domineering and possessive "my children",[11] while all the other women he has children with would talk all the time of "your children" rather than "our children". Wasn't Christine simply out of the ordinary? Of course, many women would also have

---

[11] As Momany tersely noted to the London court, "I have always wondered why the only time the Applicant talks or acts in relation to these children as if she is not their only parent is when finances are being demanded from me. And I would be in deep shit (while we were still living together) should I not be able to meet any of these financial demands: occasioning most of the verbal and/or physical provocations that are at the core of the various moving outs... [that have already been described in a footnote above]. Examples of this one-parent demeanour of the Applicant can even be seen in her always referring to them in her *Form 8* as 'my son', 'my children'; in her taking them away from Quebec without any discussion of the matter with me, in her not giving these children the chance to have their own father (who was willing to) drive them to London when they were leaving; in her registering our son in basket ball courses....[with her family name and not mine]. (I discovered this during the long weekend of 8 April 2006)." Court File N° F1162/05 (Superior Court of Justice, Family Court, London, Ontario, 2006), "Putting the Facts Straight", p. 3.

interpreted Momany's silence as anger for the rejection of his proposal. Not Christine who was waiting patiently, knowing full well that the man was merely marvelling at the depth of her uncommon *sagesse*. Momany's long-awaited response was: "Christine, dear, I just wish I wasn't leaving, and also not knowing exactly what lies ahead: I would have gone right away to see your parents now and thereafter either stay-put or only leave here with you." Now, to the experts to find out: was leaving Christine, Manjo, and Ndoungue behind in October 1984 for the UNIYAO a sensible idea on Momany's part?

Whatever those specialists may find the case with Christine to be, the plain truth, from Momany's perspective, is that child support would never have come about with her as Momany's wife since she seems to be the embodiment of an ideal spouse for him and especially regarding her emphasis on both parents being there for and with "our children". In fact, I do not know much about some of these things but I would not fear being contradicted and venture to posit that in Manjo Momany apparently failed to see the open doors while perhaps still steadfastly clinging to the closed. That locked door to marriage and family was that of Anna and the open ones being those of the Manjo girls who clearly exemplify the necessity for being there together for and with the children. Could Momany not seeing those wide-open doors in Manjo be due to the fact of not opening his eyes wide enough just as he might have failed to do and thus remained ignorant of the much love that was in the household for him?

Sistelovism: Ignorance, Revealing Pregnancy, and Perilous One-Sided Love

In the introduction of this book it has been noted that Momany did not have love within the household. But it appears as if one of his sisters (like many of his virgins) might actually have fallen so deeply in love with him at first sight and subsequently became Momany's greatest nightmare when, because of his ignorance of the real facts, he was not reciprocating her love in like manner. Do not rush to

94

wondering and blaming this sister for her natural feelings. Just remember how Momany himself instantly fell in love at first sight with his young cousin before later realizing they were cousins and, because he has also kept his feelings for her an embedded secret within himself, it also seems to have been haunting and torturing him to date. What a natural feeling, this thing called love! And what (artificial) obstacles that would often stand in the full and free expression of such natural pull and longing!

You have already noted Momany's undeclared love for the cousin that relates to his "chickening out" from being truthful and bold and from making tradition by breaking tradition. I will here be dealing with the sister's one-sided love changing to misunderstanding and war (largely attributed to Momany not "opening his four-eyes wide enough"). Not nosing around for information can be an element of failure as well as a virtue; depending on the side one looks at it (see Fossungu, 2013a: 94-96). Here, I would venture to concur that, for Momany, it has been more on the side of success than of a defect (*id*: 95). I would thus give you a major case here that makes his dislike for nosing around and his instinctive powers very splendid parts of success/failure. I am inclined to think that Momany's instinctive powers come to make up for his not nosing around for information; information that could be both constructive and destructive. In the particular case of Momany's favourite sibling, Josephine, it would have been very catastrophic in a sense. But, again, also look at the other side of the coin later, since some experts claim rightly or wrongly that there are always two sides to a story.

To begin with, bearing the same family name with him as she did, there was just no reason for Momany to be asking questions as to Josephine's paternity, except he was the perpetual noser-for-information. Momany only knew Josephine (the first daughter of his mother) was not his papa's biological daughter when she had been impregnated by one of their tenants in Yoke (these Yoke tenants again!). The man was trying to arrange marrying her and their mother was kind of trying to complicate matters. When their papa stepped in (Momany is not quite sure what he did; only sure of the fact that), both mother and daughter openly and stiffly questioned his authority in putting himself in the matter when he was not Josephine's biological father. The revelation was truly a bombshell for Momany because a lot of puzzling things that had occurred until then speedily began to take some shape. Despite the onslaught from Josephine and all the flashback after her paternity bombshell, Momany kept everything to himself and still maintained (one-sided) normality with Josephine. As a larger picture person, you develop a long memory for good deeds and a very short memory for bad ones. Remember from chapter 1 above that Josephine was the only one in the household that was not pestering Momany with the MTU nickname and that she always has been his favourite sibling. Whether she was or was not linked to him by blood, according to Momany, was not then to be important in defining his interaction with her (quite apart from her also being part of "the greatest number of persons possible"); even though that new knowledge explained certain things that were, until then, strange or inexplicable.

When pregnancy brought the news of Josephine's paternity, it then dawned on Momany that Josephine might actually have been so deeply in love with him and (because he was unintentionally not countering her love) had become so bitterly spiteful in his regard. Otherwise, what else would be responsible for this bizarre behaviour of your beloved *sister* that you have hardly seen with another man? She then brings a man one night into your room (in Muyuka in which you both often spent long evening hours together). Despite that the man is protesting since you are right there, she insists on and actually has sex with the man on the same bed where you are lying "fast asleep". And when the man is gone she comes back and wants to spend the rest of the night there but you insist on escorting her to the main house. The next morning you meet your sister, expecting some remorse for her multiple uncalled for sexual incitement of the previous evening but all you get is some kind of triumphant smile that seems to be saying "I got you, didn't I?" In short, looking back after her paternity shock wave, countless incidents before the sex-defiance clearly pointed to the fact that Josephine had been doing everything (short of openly saying it) to have Momany be having sex with her. Numerous instances after the sex-rebelliousness also clearly indicated that that incident was the cross-over point for her because it was thereafter total warfare, unlike the previous love-fare.

For the warfare, take, for instance, their papa's countless impromptu visits to Kumba during the one year Momany spent in CCAS (Cameroon College of Arts and Sciences). They were all based on Josephine's ceaseless reports that the innocent guy was housing girls in Kumba. It was their father himself that let the Josephine-cat out of the bag the day he brought Momany's acceptance slip for the G.C.E. Advanced Level. Why would your sister be saying that about you to the father of both of you? Their father would often enter Momany's room abruptly without knocking, startling the innocent and ignorant boy concentrating on his studying. Momany was never "caught" as expected, many "Thanks" to Anna's love and understanding; and thanks also to the AAD or Annastasian Automatic Door. The insufficient money he was given for the term while studying in CCAS could also be directly linked to Josephine's reports. (But didn't Momany make something positive out of this money negative?) It would not be necessary to dwell so much on the numerous (then) unfathomable encounters with Josephine during Momany's WWMSS-Mpundu days, when he would be lovingly flanked by Susan who also happened to have been Josephine's senior (or 'big') in Cameroon Baptist Academy Muyuka before moving to WWMSS-Mpundu where Momany had met her. Imagine enthusiastically introducing your lover to your other (unknown) lover who you only know as your sister, not in the least knowing just how much pain that simple and polite act of yours is causing her! Momany can narrate some of these difficult things so well because he sees himself in the same awkward position, with the sole difference being that he (unlike Josephine) knows that his cousin (until 2013) did not know; which reduces the hurting for him.

It is most probable then that Josephine was behind the MTU Girl saga in Victoria and it is not farfetched that she did try the same with Annastasia in Yoke but got coolly brushed aside. Momany even

97

remembers Annastasia once saying to him: "I cannot believe some of the things this your sister [Josephine] says about you." She would surely have told him the "things" if Momany had asked; but he had merely responded: "Annasta [his loving way of calling this woman who loved and taught him so much], I am so happy that you don't believe lies about me because that makes my knowing the lies irrelevant." Annasta always had a remarkable way of looking at Momany when he intrigued her so much and on this particular instance that peculiar gaze was there.

Until her paternity bombshell in Yoke, Momany just never understood Josephine's wacky comportment; always still relating with her as the favourite sister that he had known her to be. Just imagine, for instance, what would have become of him without his ignorance of Josephine's true paternity. As he has rhetorically put it himself, "Would I have then easily and correctly interpreted her road signs and speedily made the necessary follow ups: especially with the handicap I had with MTU Girl? She too must surely have long held her virginity up for me to grab? Would it have been possible to say no to or retract once I had started with very charming Josephine who, like Charlotte, would surely have been always available and willing?" I cannot pretend to be of help here with the last quiz but Daouda's musical piece (*La Femme de mon Patron*) would highly suggest Momany being in a dire strait and a no. I also see in that question the easiness of pregnancy (especially the scholizyvettistic type) creeping in. Could Josephine have been a lone and genuine lover or a mere attractive setup? Would Momany's life in the household have been much more smooth-going (without love-fare ever changing into warfare) had he known the facts and reciprocated Josephine's love? Could his ignorance have been an inborn protective net against the havoc that would otherwise have ensued? Could most of these questions be reversed and applied also to Momany's undeclared love for his cousin? Could said cousin actually be Christine's soft spot with Momany? Again, was leaving Manjo for Yaoundé without Christine the correct move on Momany's part? And what could really be behind his (Yaoundé City) perplexing spouse gaffes?

Chapter 4

Are Spouse (Quest) Gaffes From Manjo To Montréal Necessarily The Handiwork Of Africanscience?

Our claim is rather that we can provide an introduction to the main approaches to political science and a balanced assessment of some of the debates and disagreements that are an appropriate feature of a discipline that has several thousand years of history behind it and many thousands of practitioners in the modern world [Stoker and Marsh, 2010: 3].

In grappling with an understanding of the links (if any) between africanscience and the spouse blunders from Manjo to Montréal, and in Yaoundé particularly, I will try digging out the numerous issues that may be involved from (1) the question of what happened to the well-known theses of many doors to happiness and of the bird in hand being worth ten in the bush, (2) whether science questioning science is four-eyesism and (3) whether one should never/always judge B from A's acts.

What Happened to the 'Many Doors to Happiness' and 'Bird in Hand' Theses?

Momany's actual quest for a wife seems to have begun and ended with Anna in Yoke. Was he so sure of and too contented with having Anna that he never foresaw the possibility of a flop and therefore woefully failed to have an adequate backup 'after-flop' plan? Could that also explain his shaky position with marriage in Manjo? Should one just sum up everything perhaps by saying that, virgiluckistic as he undeniably was/is, Momany was not meant to be lucky with women in the wife domain? Or that he is being penalized for not having taken in the one that might have been meant for him at the time she came around? And, if so, when and in what city could she have come

101

around? If Momany lost Anna through the scheming of her parents and their cohorts, why did Elizabeth or Christine who both came next in line never become his wife? There may be several similar queries and reasons but could one of them be that he let the disaster in the recent past hold him back?

Momany's attitude with women in Manjo would seem to come close to resembling his post-Alice non-committal days in the Victoria school, probably because he might have actually given up on marriage at that time? Contrary to great expectations, Elizabeth and Christine were the only girls Momany actually fell in love with in Manjo. As the initial dialogues he had with each of these ladies also clearly portray, the girls, as usual, openly lined up in their numbers for him. But these two are the only that meant anything to him there; and this not just because both gave their virginity to him (many more, he could easily detect, were equally out to do so); but mainly due to the fact that, if things took their *normal* course, it is one of these two (Christine especially) that would certainly have been Momany's wife. But what happened? Could africanscience have anything to do with it? Could the unfamiliar REC Connexion also help in dispelling or fortifying the suspicion of africanscience involvement in the matter?

The Strange REC (Rita-Elizabeth-Christine) Connexion

I will begin with Elizabeth who came first in Manjo, followed by Christine; always with the important Rita colourings. Several lessons are evoked in Elizabeth's story but the principal one to be stressed here could be that you should never let something that happened to you in the past completely determine the present and future because there may be many doors to happiness. Thus, when one door is closed many more could still be open. The Anna-door to marriage, for instance, was closed in Yoke but Elizabeth's door immediately opened wide in Manjo and yet Momany did not get in because he might have in a way still be crying over the Anna spilt milk? Was he then sort of judging Elizabeth through the Anna 99-sensical mess, and/or was it Elizabeth's mum's anti-Bangwaness that was the predominant factor? Did Elizabeth's mother's stance have to matter when the lady herself was ready and willing to overlook it? Put differently, would Momany have reacted in the same way with Anna (an Anglophone) wearing Elizabeth's (a Francophone's) shoes? If one should think this question was mainly answered in the section on the Rebellious Girl's Pregnancy Story, what about the case of respectfully bold Christine who never "rushed" to get pregnant, not even by Momany's pregnancy plan, and whose parents Momany never met?

Complexion-wise, Elizabeth reminds Momany of Rita a lot. Of course, all three (the two Manjo girls and Rita) fell for him at first sight, with only Christine "respectfully and tactically" holding back. But for the problems she rushed both of them into, Elizabeth was truly (and still is) in love with Momany and could have made an ideal wife for him, which could explain why (despite how much the Anna thing was then still hurting) he made it to Kumba the following holiday. But Christine who came to replace Elizabeth was not only so deeply in love with Momany but also extremely pleasurable to be with (like Rita). She was always lighting up his heart with her enjoyable smile, and incessantly joggling his mind with her natural sharpness, most often expertly knowing and striking the right love cord in the man. With Christine's comportment particularly, one is largely tempted to think that there is no professional anything as such. The writer of these virgins' love and understanding tale with Momany, for one, would not say that he is a professional love-story writer but here is one intended for your consumption that may become your best companion: not because it is written by a professional, but simply because its message(s) may be clearer and more useful to even professionals in the domain than professionals would have made it (them) with too much professionalism and/or pretentiousness. One of the mighty lessons (learned also from Momany's numerous virgin lovers) that I am trying to get through here, is that there could actually be nothing like being a professional before doing anything correctly or exquisitely. Like Christine and Anna vividly demonstrate (respectively) in their first kiss and love

103

letter, if you have anything to do or say, just do or say it and let others worry later about how you have done or said it.

Above all else, Christine (I am really feeling like I should rather be calling her by her love-science of christickinology) was very sure of self and believed in Momany: notwithstanding the false appearances, which might be why the AAD clicked on almost as soon as Momany had her in. In fact, if a lot of people in that town were asked to line up the girls Momany was dating in Manjo, while Elizabeth would appear on the top place, Christine might not even feature or otherwise be at the bottom. Even in class it was really hard to figure out that Christine could even be the senior English teacher's girlfriend. Yet, she, not Elizabeth (the only other love Momany had there before her), practically had the best of his one year in Manjo. Unlike Elizabeth who most often behaved like a secret police behind Momany (a sign of her insecurity?), Christine very tactically avoided ever clashing with any other girl at his place of abode, not to mention that she initially truly believed that all those attention-seeking girls were actually going out (and having sex) with Momany who still "would soon come home to me." Christine did not have to be tactical for long since Momany (guided by the AAD) had almost immediately sent every *supposed* girlfriend (including Elizabeth who still stuck like chewing gum) *packing* as soon as she was in.

Did the AAD (Annastasian Automatic Door) that Rita had perfected work against Rita herself? This question is very important because I do not know how to exactly paint this whole Momany love, understanding, and spouse-seriousness thing regarding Christine except by wondering if her being with him could even have been at the root of this man's 'strange' comportment when he surprisingly reunited with Rita, one of his greatest ingredients of success with whom he had three solid defining years in primary school. Rita and Momany met in August-September 1984 on the train from Douala to Yaoundé, while he was going to enrol in the UNIYAO. Rita was just as jolly and excited about the man as ever. She even enthusiastically suggested that Momany should take a first class section of the train so that they could have their sex that they never had during their days in Kumba. Momany was indeed thrilled about her reaction and proposal but told her that he has his special way of thanking those like her who have greatly influenced his life very positively; that having a quick sex escapade on the train was the last of things he would want to use to say thank you very much, Rita; that sex or no-sex with her, she was forever endeared in his heart; and that if sex is so important to that endearment on her part, then it will naturally come at a more appropriate situation and place. What a (weird?) man!

Rita did not seem to have quite understood Momany then but rather preferred to change the discussion; saying she had often wondered about what Momany has been doing all along with "this impossible head of yours." They talked about a lot of other things and she excused herself at a point. Momany stayed on the spot, hoping she was to return; but by the time the train arrived in Yaoundé, he had not seen Rita again and that is how they lost contact again till date; but her influence is still being felt in his life and objectives – clearly making her unforgettable to him. The question, once more, is could Rita have been very disappointed with his response? Could it have been the AAD then working against Rita herself or simply money problems that hindered Momany from going along with her first-class sex-having suggestion? Was Christine's love-and-understanding christickinologistical *grip* that much immutable in this Momany? I cannot exactly tell; but being the only one he gave his contact information (care of his dad's work address) to, and also the only one who accompanied him to the motor park the day Momany was leaving Manjo/Ndoungue for Yaoundé, it is a sort of mystery (from africanscience?) that Christine never hit the wife level. The quest for the UNIYAO and the necessity for being there together with and for the children would seem to have had a big hand in it; but what also could have been contributed by the Yaoundé City effect?

The Yaoundé City and Its Adelajonistic Spoilers

Some of the Yaoundé City effects have been largely noted by Fossungu, including the fact that Momany not only lived the longest in Yaoundé but also at a level he was ready to settle down, having enrolled for university education that had been largely haunting and hurting other "settlement" issues (Fossungu, 2013a: 118-19). Additionally, I would here say, he also had the privilege (which was a killer at the same time?), for the first time, of actually living like husband and wife with some of the ladies in this city. This talk about actually living with ladies could begin nowhere else than with Joan and not end without Adela. You can get your definition of *adelajonism* from the fact that both of them not only represent some sort of spoilers but also *those who kind of easily and inexplicably blinded Momany to the bird in hand wisdom*. Neither of them was a virgin when he met them. Both (Anglophones) were also in the UNIYAO – Joan at Momany's undergraduate years and Adela during his graduate and teaching years. Their respective "victims" (Christine and Chantal), for some strange reasons, were not only high school students at the time but also Francophones. Could Elizabeth's brandishing of the 'Anglophone Card' then have some firm base? In other words, could it be that Momany was consciously or unconsciously choosing Anglophones over Francophones? The behavioural scientists have not been duly invited for nothing and I will therefore leave that also to these experts to decide after they must have had some 'empirical data' collected from (1) Joan and the New Togetherness Bar or *Jonetobarism*, (2) the Chantal-Adela Showdown or *Chantadelamatism*, (3) *Four-Eyesism* or the clash between Sciences and (4) whether it is sane never/always to judge B from A's acts.

Mami-Watarisation or Jonetobarism?

Jonetobarism is the love and understanding philosophical terminology that describes the effects and consequences of Joan's New Togetherness Bar; the lady herself also being a generally acclaimed *mami wata*. Describing a lady as, or calling her, *mami wata* can mean one of two (or both) things, one positive the other negative. Positively, it entails that she is so beautiful to the point of defying words to be appropriately employed in painting a correct picture of her good looks and attraction. On the negative side and africanscientifically, it refers to her being this bewitching creature that is believed to live in an underwater world and regularly comes around in the form of a very beautiful woman to enchant and lure away men into its world where they are imprisoned or killed. What type of *mami wata* did Momany encounter in Yaoundé then?

Momany was already more than a month in the UNIYAO and, since leaving Manjo, Christine was always with him (as usual) and influencing almost everything he was doing. She was already his wife as far as he was concerned and he just needed to find a way to put everything in place and, in her wise words, "come and see my people and get me." Because of the vast three-year gap between his G.C.E. results and when he enrolled in the UNIYAO, Momany could not be accorded *boursea* that year. The September 1981 bombshell (see Fossungu, 2013: chapter 3) was obviously still having multiplier effects (money-wise and otherwise) up to that time and beyond. Momany had consequently moved out of the student residential quarters in Ngoa-Ékellé (where he had met straight-shooting Solomon) to a room opposite the EMIA (the Military and Armed Forces School) in Melen in order to cut cost and also to see how he could start getting ready to go for Christine during Christmas holiday or the next. It was just about a month and half after the start of the university-year; and he had been at the EMIA new residence for about two weeks. Still attempting to reduce cost, Momany decided to start taking a shortcut to campus rather than going by cab when on that fateful morning he met a Banyangi beauty, a *mami wata*, as some would say.

Momany was coming up while she was going down the hilly footpath and when he looked up and their eyes met, they both temporarily froze for a while. Momany does not know if he got it right but it seems as if he heard Christine's unique voice at that very frozen moment demanding "What is happening?" Why did he ignore

107

that very lovely and familiar voice? Why? Coming out of the freeze, Momany heard himself saying aloud "What a beauty!" and the lady (still motionlessly standing there) just smiling very appetizingly like Chantal would do some years later. He then advanced deliberately and stopped in front of the ebony-black slender and tall smiling lady and said: "Frankly, I would not mind skipping my classes today just to have a word with you." Still smiling, she indicated: "But you have already had more than a word; go to class then." Was Momany already possessed or what? He asked for her name, telling her his; as well as what she was studying, indicating he was in law. The blindingly charming beauty brightened up more and said she was Joan, also reading law. So could he have a chat with her somewhere more comfortable? She said she was hurrying to somewhere and he then suggested her showing him where she lives or he shows her where he lives "so that one of us at least knows where to find the other." "What for?" she demanded; and Momany responded with "What for? You mean to tell me that you don't feel anything? Please let's stop pretending and behaving childishly." Before she could say a thing further, he firmly took hold of her hand and said: "Just show me your place or see mine."

Momany was surprised that they were living in the same area. As they had to pass his place to reach hers, he took Joan to his. She could not just stop talking about his room's cleanliness, tidiness, arrangement, comfort and, above all, the genre of music that automatically started with the opening of the door. She was very impressed with Momany's cooking too, although at first complimenting but "your girlfriend [who] cooks well". He accepted her compliments "on Joan's behalf", saying "I am very sure you did the cooking even before I had seen and brought you here today." That is a very funny way of telling me you don't have a girlfriend, she observed. Momany again put in a small correction, indicating that she should substitute "don't" with "didn't". She simply shook her head, smiling lovingly and said "I've really gotten into something." They stayed almost the whole day, 'forgetting' completely that Joan had been hurrying to somewhere. From that day on they became as

108

inseparable as blood and flesh, practically living together, going to school together, and reading together.

As indicated already, Joan was not a virgin like the others but she was a first in her own right since Momany had never before enjoyed such togetherness with any other woman and this cohabitation sweetly lasted for close to two years; therefore making Joan come behind only Rita and Anna in duration. Joan was clearly factored into Solomon's coinage of Momany's *Power* nickname since (from the Presbyterian college they both attended in Bessong-Abang in South West Region) Solomon had known the type of Susan-like lady Joan was. Victoria or Limbe soon became Joan's popular holiday town and Momany also got to know a lot of her relatives there. Everyone, including his parents and siblings as well as hers, knew Joan and Momany were headed for the altar to tie the knot. To Momany, it was just a matter of waiting for their graduation. Everything seemed to be rolling well and in the right direction until Joan simply left Momany for another guy who had just passed into the National School of Administration and Magistracy (ENAM).

Joan, like Anna, had thus set her own new bar of togetherness and left. This jonetobarism had not only forward but also backward effects. Backwardly, it had kind of effaced the memory of the Manjo ladies, Christine (and Elizabeth). Life with Joan had literally made Momany to stop communication with Christine. Forwardly, it was then kind of hard to have another relationship that fell below the Joan-Bar, especially with those who could not move in or come as frequently such as Chantal, Odilia, and Yvette. The Joan tale is surely not going to vanish without a particularly difficult Question Time that must necessarily drag on till and into the *Four-Eyesing* of the AAD below. Did the Joan-Bar or jonetobarism also work against Joan herself? That is, was the fact that Momany was already virtually living with her as husband and wife impinging on his not being in a hurry to formalize a marriage relationship? Could the post-Joan Odilia haste that became very fatal, as well as Christine's reasoning on the pregnancy-before-marriage plan, not all be indicating an affirmative? Could the advice, especially from christickinology, then

109

be: Don't start living as husband and wife until you are husband and wife? Did Christine's sensible reasoning on the pregnancy plan also work against her? That is, would Joan have even come into the scene, let alone completely obliterating her, if Christine was then carrying "our child" with Momany?

Was Joan not right then in calling it quits and going after what she thought was readily available, especially as the ENAM guy's future then seemed brighter than Momany's? Should Momany blame Joan for leaving him when he fully understands how she had also abruptly left a man who was then working in a Yaoundé bank for Momany? Could it not be that she left the banker because she found something in Momany then that she was not getting from the banker? Is this leaving one for the other what made Anna and others (in chapter 2) to describe girls of Joan's ethnic group as *ashawo*? Quite apart from this *epithetization* being like judging B from A's acts, would Momany's for-no-apparent-reason leaving of Christine for Joan not then also be similarly defined as harlotry or *ashawonism*? Perhaps Momany waited for too long and Joan was sort of tired of the wait? Why did she not bring the issue up, if that was the case? Would there have been love and understanding between these two 'hypnotic' lovers? Were both lovers here not kind of suffering from nonoselfism; that is, their not really knowing what they wanted? And why did Joan try to come back to Momany two years later, without admitting her error but instead behaving as if he was the one to be apologizing to her?

The foregoing queries may appear to be superfluous but are essential because losing Joan was very painful and shocking to Momany; making hard reality of all the Leo Sayer songs (especially *Sea of Heartbreak* and *No Business like Love Business*) that had become the duo's favourite tunes. There were indeed lots of lonely nights and tears on Momany's pillow but he concentrated (difficult as it plainly was) on passing his exams to the third year and (thanks to the Ritaian crisebacology) he made it flying high as usual, with Joan repeating. For success at the time, Momany had also largely fallen back and invoked the Anna era for strength; vigour that was constantly and unfailingly being dragged down by the unadorned guilt in regard of Christine. Was this not the time to go back looking for Christine and asking for pardon and a fresh start with her? Would she still be there after the two years of silence, and what was Momany to give as explanation that would not be a lie? The Anna saga was just as painful but Momany could then grasp its workings even without knowing what precisely they were. But the Joan tale was kind of baffling him a lot. First, unlike Anna, Joan never gave any reason for leaving. Second, the Ritaian crisebacology had greatly aided him from day one with Joan and he had been excelling academically and otherwise; but at this time that Joan was gone what was there to draw from Rita?

Only more puzzlement, indeed, and this is where the Joan story really flummoxes, pushing a lot of people sometimes to want to agree with one arm of the Four-Eyes Theorists who rush to africanscience for easy and simplistic explications. Notwithstanding the monument that Rita has been and still is in his life, Momany could not give in to her request on the train in August-September 1984, most likely because of money problems or of Christine's wise and respectful bold love? If because of the latter, how come then that around November 1984 Momany was the one ignoring that familiar magical voice and jumping at Joan (then a complete stranger to him), and so even after all the solid arrangements he had with the same Christine before leaving Manjo for Yaoundé? Even more significantly, where exactly had the AAD gone to this time, not to be there looking out for Christine? Why did Momany not also think of the bird in hand adage concerning Christine? And why was this same bird-in-hand lesson not learnt by the time Chantal also came into the scene? The bird in hand idiom, like the AAD, also (in)explicably failed Chantal. Was jonetobarism, perhaps, also what principally tilted the weight against Chantal and in favour of Adela?

Chantadelamatism or the Decision that Was Not Made

Adela would appear to have had the hidden disadvantage of jonetobarism advantaging her; or could her advantage instead be tied to the Elizabethan anglocardism? This is Yaoundé, five years after Momany left Manjo and christickinology. Adela is Mbo, very "hot" indeed, and would easily win a model contest even in America; otherwise, she would not be in this book. But if there is any memory of Adela, it is not because of the wonderful love-and-understanding life Momany had with her but rather because of the breathtaking wife-to-be the man kind of enigmatically left for her. I am talking about Chantal, another Dschang lady like Jane. I cannot really paint a complete portrait of Chantal without one side of the ambiguous *mami-wata* expression but, put briefly, she is the kind of woman that would turn heads like Chris de Burgh's Lady in Red, not only because of her physical beauty. Chantal also has this air of royalty around her and carries herself around as no other woman Momany has known. He remembers vibrantly the reaction of his own brother who seldom shows his emotion on this as other matters. After having met Chantal, said brother could not help asking right away to know where Momany had found 'this Blood'. Describing a woman with this phrase in Cameroon simply means that one cannot exactly find the right words to put on her beauty and attractiveness (positive *mamiwatarisation* physically, to be exact). One of Momany's sisters has had many occasions to meet his female friends, some of whom have even been her own friends or classmates. Also talking very positively about Chantal, said sister had hoped "that this was the end of your wife search." But it would seem that love that is too much (if any is ever too much) scarcely lasts too long. Here are Chantal's own last words to Momany: *C'est bien toi qui me fais ça, mon Roi?* – My King, I just can't believe you are the one doing this to me. These words would forever remain with Momany, haunting him every day and night as much as he has been brutally hurt by Anna's in her last letter.

When Momany first set eyes on Chantal, it was just like re-meeting Anna (without the trance-evoking letter) but with a face-to-face daze all the same, almost identical to the one in the Letia

Cousilovism. There she was sitting right in front of him, in a class where there were so many pretty and attention-seeking girls. Momany temporarily lost his cool and senses when his eyes fell on her; only being awakened by her very telling smile. It was simply magical and everyone in class seemed to have picked up the palpably obvious mutual current flow that took place. At the end of the school day (that he couldn't wait to come) Momany asked Chantal if he could give her a ride – not even knowing where she was heading to. When she said it was alright, he counted himself very fortunate but even luckier when she decided to come on board right there in full view of all rather than wait for him elsewhere, away from the college.

Welcome then to the World of *Chantomapheticism*. The first chat with Chantal was not only very romantic; it was prophetic as well. Her beauty was so blinding that Momany of all people almost found himself at a loss beginning the conversation once they were ready to talk one on one. As he looked into her eyes that were very confidently and understandingly looking into his, Momany felt like Chantal was reading him like an open book. Stuck and almost not knowing how to start, he then said simply that "I had just asked you to come with me because I have this feeling from deep inside me that you are the perfect queen for my kingdom." She did not even hesitate before replying: "I can see you're a prince; but if you have a kingdom of your own, then I would very much like to live there." Momany was still trying to come to grips with what she said at the beginning (how did she know?) when she added: "I'd like to be your queen, not one of your queens." He sort of woke up from the spell that her initial words had thrown him into and simply said "Guaranteed." Imagine all this conversation in the original language through which it was oozing out, French; a language well known for its romantic characteristics. Remember too that this is their first day of ever meeting each other and that beautifully-blinding Chantal is Momany's student but she was not acting as if that was the case. He does not remember pulling her into his arms but they were deep in embrace when he heard her saying in his ear: "My King, I hope this is as real as I think it is." "Me too" was the response. Momany felt so overwhelmingly complete from that moment. He felt terribly whole from that special hug. But how could such a wholesome and satisfying feeling then become a big problem?

Chantal is not the talking type but more of the listening kind. She was simply so sweet and Momany had fallen so deeply in love with her. He cannot even begin to use an adequate amount of words to say how completely nourishing he felt with Chantal except to just say "I wanted to meet her parents in order to traditionally (if not officially) bring her home. I just could not afford a whole day without seeing this woman. Her unique smile, her way of seeming to know what I am thinking, like Mami Regina, her just making me completely complete. It [chantomapheticism] was simply killing me softly." Three types of marriages are recognized in Cameroon: customary, religious, and official. It is one's choice to go through any or all of them but, usually, most people only proceed with the others in church/mosque and in the mayor's office (often combined) after the customary rites have been fulfilled. That explains why Momany wanted to meet Chantal's parents "in order to traditionally (if not officially) bring her home." But the chained demon in Momany was turned loose by Chantal not being "comfortable" with introducing him to the uncle and aunty she said she was living with in Yaoundé, her parents having residence in Dschang in the West Region. During school term the problem did not stiffly surface because he still saw her every day; but not during holiday. Although Chantal did her best to visit during weekends on holiday, Momany did not seem to see why he could not see Chantal when he wanted to; a thing that must have pushed him in the first place to even see Adela. A drowning man, they say, would cling on anything, even onto a snake, to stay afloat?

I do not know but I do not see any other way of explaining this man's attitude when both ladies met in his apartment a few days after his *cocklering* or winning-over Adela who was then virtually jonetobarring or moving in. A high school student then, Chantal was obviously disturbed thrice finding Adela there but always remained very classy and cool whereas Adela (who was then some sort of encroaching on the other's territory) often kept fuming around and acting like a real primary school pupil, not the university student that she was. The third consecutive time was unquestionably decision time for Momany because it was exceedingly obvious that one of the two ladies must have to go; but did he choose? Could his not being able to see Chantal every time he wanted to, actually have caused his losing her when all the evidence was there to show him the way to retaining but her? Was her classy and cool behaviour also consonant with her degree of love and acceptance to be his queen and not one of his queens? Put differently, could it be that his stubborn side was 99-sensically waiting for Chantal to at least stage a fight over him?

Christine's unique case aside, one can say that if Momany has ever personally blown his relationship with any woman for no sanely explainable reason, this would be the second. Shouldn't one think that at the very moment that Momany needed his clock-ticking head so badly it failed him? Why? And why could he not have then made good use of the adage 'A bird in hand is worth ten in the bush'? By the way, which of the birds was then really in the hand and which in the bush? Momany clearly had the best opportunity to let us know this. Rather, he hesitated, hesitated, and hesitated in making a firm choice between two people that rarely had anything in common, and even devastatingly so as Momany himself clearly says that "something so powerful was shouting inside my head 'Chantal is your woman, don't be a fool. Go but for her.' Indeed, it was a fatal hesitation, as Chris de Burgh would say. Why did I need to be with Chantal so much that it kind of clouded my love for her in a way?" Again, I cannot quite answer that query, wisely turning it over to my panel of experts; but perhaps children like Momany that have grown up without getting the motherly love (that comes with growing in the bosom of their biological mother) get into this 'madness' when they really love a woman? Does it in fact come down to jonetobarism or to the Elizabeth Anglophone Card? What valuable lessons can be drawn from the Christine and Chantal episodes? Any place in these many spouse-gaffes for africanscience?

Is Science Questioning Science Four-Eyesism?

This book is not out to deny the existence of witchcraft or what it describes as africanscience because it is just as real as 'European Science'. But I think questions have to be stiffly raised over this notorious tendency to over see it as belying everything we consider hard to explicate. For instance, the fact that the AAD failed to cover Christine of all people (and Chantal) certainly raises some very important love and understanding questions. But it would seem preposterous to simply conclude that some of Momany's relations in the village or elsewhere are doing this or that with witchcraft and that is why he is having this or that spouse issues. Among the said queries evoked on the AAD, some observers could also ask about what AAD-confined Momany is like without the AAD; that is, when he is not in love? This appears to be an apt question and I found it helpful to bring it to the attention of Momany whose approach to it was: "I suppose you are writing about the philosophy of love [and understanding], not the philosophy of no-love situations." That is a real piece of Momanysm, is it? Let us now find out what the four-eyes experts would think about it, carefully bearing in mind the double-sided nature of four-eyesism.

Four-Eyesing AAD Absence and Failures

A set of the critics called **the Quick-Jumpers** would levy the following blame. Momany's response may be logical, they admit; but they think it could be because we tend to want to over 'compartmentalize' life that there is failure to four-eyesly visualize that what happens during those 'no-love situations' could and do often enormously impact on the 'love philosophy's happenings'. Would that be like saying with Stoker and Marsh (2010: 6) that "science should be interested not only in understanding 'what is', it should also be concerned with the normative issues of 'what should be'"? That advice too could be very important in this debate between four-eyesers "on both sides of the Atlantic" (Hay and Wincott, 1998: 975); although I think said theorists (quick jumpers) are simply explaining that it is because of the "love and no-love"

116

compartmentalization (just as the theory-practice, and particular-approach, wrangling[12]) that we often find some of the incidents to be inexplicable and, therefore, are quick to attribute them to africanscience. Furthermore, they would question, why does Momany leave room for speculation (by evading?) when he could have directly responded to the question? So, they still want know, is Momany a real Casanova between AADs?

They claim that this enquiry of theirs is important to be addressed not just because it leads to knowledge of what happens when Momany is not in love. It also crucially enhances our understanding of why AAD did not protect those (like Christine and Chantal) that we consider deserving of its protection; thus, excluding the rush to attribute seemingly inexplicable occurrences to africanscience. As to how this period could impact on the other, they cite a barrage of situations to sustain their speculation. Among these are the following they insist on: You heard Anna's first love letter talking about and condemning the several girls that did not merit Momany's valuable time and energy. Could some of such girls not be of the Casanova-period? And what happened to the transition from Susan to Anna? Could the Casanova-period speculation not also explain the attitude of Momany's friend, Odilia's sister? Could his friend here not have simply been protecting her junior sister from the Casanova-period monster she might well know of? What about Jane's Big that Jane herself knew Momany once dated and from whom she was hiding? Wasn't Momany even actually enjoying having all the Yoke camp girls before Annastasia got him pinned down? Would *fidatydoning* (first-day tying-down) lovers like Rita and Elizabeth not also be some sort of unparalleled blessings to Momany (the Casanova), as they also theorize?

Yes, of course, Rita fidatydoned him in Kumba and Elizabeth from Kumba also had him pinned down from day one in Manjo until

---

12 "We close by returning to the issue of variety within political science by arguing that diversity should be a cause for celebration rather than concern" (Stoker and Marsh, 2010: 6)

117

Christine respectfully and boldly took over, beating both 'Kumba' ladies in a matchless way (in the *Strange REC Connexion*). Yet, Christine (with her praiseworthy christickinology) could not similarly trounce the complete-stranger *mami wata* in Yaoundé? In other words, their argument goes, are you telling us and expecting us to really believe that there was no actual negative mami-watarization or africanscience when the respectfully bold girl got so near to the *spouseology* (wife) finish-line but did not actually cross it simply because of some little doubt (see *chrichantism* below) raised in Momany? Come on! This is the normal quick query of the easy-way thinkers who, oxymoronically, do not quite seem to see easy explanations. The quick-jumping (or easy-way) critics have obviously had their day in court but I cannot quick-jump to condemning their idea since "no idea that is aired is useless. What I think is unfruitful is an idea that is not aired or made known. Sometimes (if not often) it takes a small or little idea from one head to provoke or nourish a grand or big idea from another head" (Fossungu, 2013a: 124-25).

But, again, we often hear that there are two sides to any good story. It may now be the time and turn of the critics' critics or those who civilize and beautify the art of (literary) criticism in the same way as opposition political parties are supposed to do to politics everywhere (except in Africa?). The other groups of the four-eyesers known as **the Civilizers or Beautifiers** have been patiently waiting and the floor is now theirs. This other group would begin by wanting to know why we should now categorize and speculate on Momany's answer to a question if we have to believe other things he has told us before (I will come back to this later). Moreover, they ask, would stressing on the Casanova period not be ignoring the important fact that Momany is not the ladies' man only during that period, but always – which might even be the reason for the AAD gift from nature in the first place? What about the roles of the rare qualities that, unlike Casanova's (sex), do particularly turn him on in a woman? Are we now to suppose that, simply because he is having no real lover (and don't forget we are here also forgetting the reason why he is then not having one), he will just jump into bed with any woman

118

who presents herself to him? If so, then what is there to stop him from doing same even while having a real lover; and what makes such real lover one? Beautiful beautifiers, is all I can say here.

The civilizers or beautifiers clearly are not yet done with the easy-wayers. As they further ask, why also categorize his response as evasive unless we are behaving like the social scientist who refuses to publish new findings simply because the empirical data supporting it did not tie with what s/he started out intending to prove or falsify; or who simply engages in unethically fabricating empirical data to suit his/her taste like the Dutch university professor called Dederik Stapels (see Bhattacharjee, 2013). Wouldn't that also be indicative of the fact that we already had an answer for him like is the case with African dictators and journalistic interview questions? For those of you who do not quite know this *journadictationalism* story, these civilizers would quickly point to Fossungu (1998) or directly to the concerned journalist himself (Eric Chinje) who is happily still alive and could better talk about the ordeal of any such professionals that would dare to ask said tyrants anything outside the list of questions handed to them beforehand. Therefore, as these beautifying four-eyesers inquire, why keep condemning these dictators when we cannot comport ourselves any different from them?

As the beautifiers have then pointedly indicated to the others on the opposing side, no human being is an angel; and wouldn't the fact that even angels have their flaws be evidenced by the heavenly war in Milton's *Paradise Lost*? To these civilizers then, we should perhaps just stop trying to find fault where none might actually exist and simply heed to Sam's Mother's bag-carrying advice (see Fossungu (2013a: 40) and know that Momany is exceptional in the domain and thus valuably learn something from his moving love and understanding experiences. These critics' critics might be quite right and it looks very much like some of them have discovered that many readers might not quite grasp the arguments in this book without a complete and comprehensive perusal of *Africans in Canada: Blending Canadian and African Lifestyles?* (2013) authored by "Fossungu [who, perhaps] is writing an on-going journal or memoir" (Codling, 2013). For the

119

purpose of learning from said experiences, therefore, I would rather rephrase the first bunch of critics (the quick-jumpers) and say Momany's response is philosophical and thus also attempt "philosophizing" on and through the AAD's two failure-versions of *Chrichantism* and of *Scholadela Assumption.*

Chrichantism and the Scholadela Assumption

Chrichantism: Christine and Chantal are obviously behind this terminology. Remember always that the AAD only encircles and unchangeably shields said lover with Momany's belief in her bold, true, and reciprocal love; meaning therefore that any doubt as to that trust would sort of de-encircle and firm protection would then be lost. Might Christine's not going along with his well-intentioned pregnancy plan not have done just that? Bringing it back down to christickinologizing, was this not like Christine not being sure of Momany's immense love for her while he is away from her? Is this not a real possibility? Since the duo both seem to 'share the same clock-ticking head', could this same 'scientific' thinking not be behind Christine's response to the pregnancy plan? Would their narrative be indicative that two persons with almost the same personality traits would hardly be good matches in some of these matters? Is this not also an implicit theory in the Schemer vs. Schemer scenario? That is to say that like poles repel, as physics tells us? In short, that Schola would have woefully failed in her schemes if Momany was also a schemer?

Some critics of chrichantism may find Momany's money situation in Yaoundé (his not being granted *bourse* or *epsi*) as being largely responsible for the Joan *mami wata* incident (as it was for the Rita train sex proposal?), not the *Chrichant Doubt Raiser* (CDR). That being so, the question would then become: Was Momany at the time of chantadelamatism (he was teaching in both UNIYAO and Chantal's high school, plus his *epsi* for doctoral programme) also having the same money issues? Might the same CDR not have applied to Chantal's reluctance to introduce him to her Yaoundé relations, leading to the 'release of the demon in him', fortified by her not putting up a fight with Adela over him (as anxiously sought for by his 'stubborn side')? Yes, Adela is almost everywhere *adelaying* as she also brings in the notorious *scholadela assumption* which ignores how one arm of the AAD's dooractionism functions.

The Scholadela Assumption: The AAD seems to have worked in regard of Schola just like it did concerning Adela; these two also being the only two women to whom Momany has dedicated two of his Master's researches! How much he must have loved each of them (as he does to any woman that enjoys the gift's dooractionism)! As you already know, the AAD effect on Momany is that he concentrates his love on the person in question to the (complete) exclusion of all others. Most women (as men, with necessary substitution) usually then easily and swiftly conclude or assume that, with this degree of loving and concentration, Momany (like most deep lovers) has reached the point of no return; and, therefore, they can do whatever they like. After all, is he not already firmly locked up or enslaved in their lovely-fortified prison?

Schola and Adela, who are behind the terminology, are clean and clear cases of this *scholadela assumption*. The latter had unequivocally indicated, for instance, to a friend of hers that was very much worrying about what would happen if her *massa* (Momany) found out the games she was then playing behind his unsuspecting back: "My friend, why do you worry yourself too much? Prof [her own preferred nickname for Momany] loves me too much; even to an extent that I now know I can go to the moon and come back and he will still always be there calmly waiting for me." Was she here not also forgetting the contradictions in 'Absence makes the heart grow fonder' and 'Out of sight, out of mind' idioms? Schola would also be heard similarly boasting around to her friends especially in Montréal in various versions; including specifically how she knows Momany "will always be following me around like my dog, especially now that I have a professional job." Also remember Joan coming back two years later and expecting Momany to be apologizing to her and begging her back into his crushed heart for a subsequent crushing;

and then "going wacko" when that was not actually happening. That snap-shot gives you a lucid picture of how most women who claim they are in love with Momany just do not have a clue of who he really is. Is love without such understanding love?

What most people (including said women) just do not know is that the AAD liberates Momany in the same way as it imprisons the *mulomon* ('multiple-lovers-mongering') demon in him. They thus forget or do not realize that one of the A's in the AAD means that no real effort is required on Momany's part for the dooractionism: except his belief in or doubt of real reciprocal love that tickles the switch. It is interesting finding out when, for Schola specifically, that switch-tickling moment occurred; and what must have led to it, and thus letting Momany's demon free. Was Schola then overtaken and surprised on finding Momany not to be 'dogging' around her? Could the famous London court suit not be her own way of "going wacko" as well as a means of testing just how much the 'dog' would still be tailing her? Without the scholadela assumption theory, how else do you explain her numerous "eyes and ears all over" that are still nosing for information in the dog's regard until date? As to what must be responsible for the tickling of *dooractionism*, there are so many things from the discussion in chapter 3 above that one can hardly pin-point any particular incident(s). But the capagivists can help us grasp the time issue in this scholadela assumption narrative.

Capagivism: Time too is hard to precise. But I think it must certainly have been any time before June 2004, date on which Queenta sort of very easily made her way into Momany's heart of gold, as seen below in *flaviqueenism*. This date thesis could be firmly rooted; otherwise, it would be really hard to explain why, alone for four years in Montréal, Momany never gave in to the numerous women but did so while under the same roof with Schola. It is significant that some of unsuccessful women during the alone-time even used *capagivism* (the strategy of "giving Canadian papers" through marriage) to sort of find their way into his heart of gold. Momany particularly remembers two of said capagivistic ladies (one from the Caribbean and the other, a white and '*québeçoise de source*')

122

because of their intriguing reactions to his not being vulnerable even to *capagivism* that most people would themselves be searching very hard and hardly finding. The first Caribbean capagivist had stated: "I just cannot understand you African men. I am right here with you giving you my all and you're only thinking of a thing you left back faraway in Africa? How come you African men never even learn when these women of yours you are so keen on bringing over always get here and screw you up?" Of course, Momany certainly did not particularly like her generalisation about African women and made that clear to her; but was she not chantomophetically (charmingly and prophetically) right about Schola?

The second had particularly reminded Momany about scholizyvettism. Having failed with the capagivism thing, she said: "Okay, I don't exactly know why I am feeling this much for and wanting to be with you. Since you do not want to forget about your African woman, I think I can still live with just replacing her until she gets here. Can I get that, please?" Momany's intuitive response simply was "I've already had a lot of complications in my life with pregnancies that are not mutually planned." To her response-question "Are all African men as intelligent as you?" Momany responded: "I wish I was 'All African Men' to correctly answer your question. As you can see, I'm just one of them." The look on this white lady's face at this point was not much different from Annasta's after the 'Josephine Unbelievable Things' dialogue in the last chapter. Now, absent the scholadela assumption that is directly drawn from clean-and-clear onsilovundism, would it not be solely paradoxical that women would be ceaselessly attempting to use capagivism and some versions of scholizyvettism in order to find their way into Momany's heart of gold and marriage; but Schola who is already firmly into both of these would rather be using same 'instruments' to screw up the man (without whom she never would have acquired her own 'capagivistic powers')? What then would you think must have been going through Momany's mind when 'your African woman' eventually got to Canada and was using "papers" and "pregnancies" the way she did? And what else is put on the discussion table by chantadelamatism?

Some of Chantadelamatism's Lessons

Chantadelamatism brings in many other lessons, including that of not letting others make your decision for you. But its other lesson that needs to be specifically highlighted here again for Schola and her parents could be the fact that uncles, aunts, etc. can never replace a child's living parents as they would seem to think. Schola is apparently feeling the consequences of the scholadela assumption and is ruthlessly punishing the children for that; narrow-mindedly thinking that it is their father she is penalising. I am made to understand that in March 2012, Schola was in Montréal with the two children on a Wednesday and putting up at her brother's. Momany wanted to have them on Friday evening so they could spend at least a night or two. But she put these words in the children's mouth: "They say they cannot come and stay at your place because they are not used to your wife." Who is actually speaking here? It is for sure small-mindedness and a vinegary scholadelassumptionist. So, when are these children ever going to get used to "Momany's wife" *before* they start coming?

Schola finally and very inconsiderately left Montréal without Momany seeing the children; again, because she was bent on trying to make him bitter when, contrary to the arrangement they had on the phone for him to have them even for a few hours on Saturday, Schola never brought them down when Momany rang the door bell. She later insisted on the phone that the man should have come up to her brother's apartment to get the children. As Momany has wondered about it, "I had no business going up, not that Eugene and I have any problem. We often meet and exchange greetings. We have been in Montréal for quite a while and he has never been to where I live; which is not a problem at all to me. But what was Schola's motive for insisting that I should come into his apartment when she would rather give but her own London cell phone number (and not Eugene's home phone in Montréal) for me to use in calling back?"

124

I have to reiterate without fear of being repetitive that there is clear reinforcement from chantadelamatism to the effect that no aunt or uncle can ever replace Schola or Momany to the two children they have together. There are things that their daughter, for example, would not feel comfortable discussing with her uncle or aunt but instead with Schola or Momany (her parents). Here clearly attesting is young and beautiful Chantal who had not only found a prospective husband but also someone she apparently loved so dearly and who loved her as well in return. But everything went off track solely because this lady was not *comfortable* with the aunt or uncle she was living with at the time. Similarly, Elizabeth, the rebellious girl, never introduced Momany to the relations with whom she was living in Manjo but quickly did so to her parents far away in Kumba. With Chantal chrichantly gone, Adela also made up the same uncomfortableness excuses regarding her uncle and aunt in Yaoundé but Momany did not have a major problem with that, probably because she was then up to jonetobarism?

But could some of these *uncomfortableness* excuses not also be conveniently interpreted as evidence of nonoselfism (or the art of not knowing oneself and what one really wants): or of the lack of love and understanding? This question is so apt and cuts across like a sharp knife because, as Momany actually found out later in Adela's case, those uncle and aunt turned out to be her other men at whose street entrances he used to drop her off! No one-sided blame here, please. Could Adela's not dropping these other men (if they were there before Momany) or taking them up being already with him, not be because she might have thought Momany too was still seeing Chantal – since he never made a clean and clear decisional choice between the two of them? Whatever Adela's actual thinking, her scholadelassumptionistic comportment is a great lesson in insults and in double-talking or lies that Momany has also had to learn from the women with whom he has children, and especially Schola (the ideal woman he thought he eventually married) who arrived in Canada in 1999 with a signification of family that undoubtedly defies both Africa's and Canada's. Yet, as some perplexed critics want to know,

125

Momany is known to have stubbornly refused to jump to judging B from A's acts, including ignoring the Anglophone-Francophone stuff?

Flaviqueenism: Is It Sane Never/Always to Judge B from A's Acts?

Flavie (the common law spouse), like Queenta (the intelligent nurse), could easily represent the fact that Momany has learned not to judge B from A's acts because most people in his shoes that have not done such learning would hardly want to even talk about marriage again (let alone sponsoring the person) after "the Scholastica surprising family definitional mess in Canada" (Fossungu, 2013a: 115) that is now crowned with addictive 'family' blackmail and nosing for information in Momany's regard. An instance of the condemned scholaparentism that would appear to belie all this could be picked from Momany's June 2004 visit to Cameroon, a case that also conveniently gives you a taste of flaviqueenism, an almost incurable disease that not only Schola but also her mother would be suffering from.

During said visit, Momany's mother-in-law (without even mentioning the money the man had sent to her when her husband died), declared to Momany that he was not right in refusing her daughter (Schola) from schooling. It is not worth the waste of time on the veracity or otherwise of her statements; but just listening to her saying this told Momany a lot more about her. First, that she has such a short or no memory for good deeds, which is very normal with the scheming and ungrateful types. Who is responsible for making her daughter and all of them for that matter what they are today? This woman was here not even finding out what had happened between her daughter and the man but had already taken her daughter's gossip and lies (if not even actually her very own) as gospel truth and was spreading them around like dry season bush fire. I quite understand that Momany does not like judging someone from another's actions. But would anyone who says here 'Like mother like daughter' be wrong? I will thus continue discussing 'Not Judging' through flaviqueenism; with the nurse who came first before

126

the common law partner that inappropriately or flaviqueenically filled the place the first failed to conveniently or christickinologically occupy.

The Intelligent Nurse

Momany had just arrived Nwangong (his village) from Canada in June 2004 for an unplanned trip to attend to his sick birth mother. Later that evening he met Queenta (a Bafut from North West Region) in the health post, being operated in a portion of his father's house. She was the village nurse at the time and they greeted each other and, as they talked, Momany requested an interview with her since he had his video and other cameras as usual and was very much thinking of how to help improve the services she was rendering to the village community. He was not at all, not even remotely, thinking about her in any terms other than the professional nurse that she was. She happily accorded the interview and Momany was happy too since not many people in her situation would want to be embarrassed with such an impromptu interview. He immediately got the camera set and rolling.

The interviewer was really struck by the interviewee's mastery of her subject and domain; the confidence in her; her detailed but straightforward explications of the technicalities of her trade; the extremely intelligent way she articulated her points; the way she loved what she was doing; and her earnest desire to help people, be it in the village or city setting; and, finally, the bold way she was looking straight at him during the entire interview. This was the first time they ever were meeting each other and it certainly did not begin as a love story but by the time it ended it was surely one. By the time Momany had thanked Queenta for according him the privileged enlightenment and ended the interview, there was no doubt in the mind of either of them that they had been very rapidly falling for each other. Action then quickly took over from words.

If the evening before he had only started falling for Queenta, by morning Momany was swept away. Yes, you are absolutely right, it is 2004, with Momany still being a 'married man' under the same roof.

But he could clearly not remember the last time he had anything like that from his own wife who had arrived in Canada in April 1999 (after four years of 'consensual' separation). Of course, it is not just about the sex that was so hot that, starting as protected, ended being unprotected. But also the breakfast that was already set up, warm bath water ready, shoes cleaned and dirty clothes washed, by the time Momany got out of bed. In the man's own proper moving words, "If I had not already planned to provide the village with a generator, I would still have made that decision that morning. In short, that June morning I felt like I could marry again although I did not make any promises to Queenta to that effect then. It came a few years later, not simply because of the treats just described but solely because, from the interview, she seemed to share my objective of making life more worthwhile for many people without restrictions to certain relationships and places." You can then see why Queenta and Momany had been heading for marriage despite all what was being said about her even by members of his extended royal family; and also notwithstanding some of Schola's "eyes and ears" having thereafter chased her out of Nwangong, as has become traditional for them to do.

What happened then that Queenta never got into spouseology? Nonoselfism is a big problem; and resulting from it is flaviqueenism that can be defined as this short-ranged, scheming, and scholadelastically-assumed comportment. In short, the staggering absence of love and understanding, I think. Momany went to Cameroon in January 2007 to formalize things with Queenta's family and almost got killed by thieves in Bonaberi, Douala. After the problems that successively followed on his return to Canada, he sadly realized Queenta did not quite know what she wanted, especially as she does not embrace the bitter truth without getting bitter, nor look at the larger picture of things. For instance, when Momany notified her at the close of 2007 that the project for their (her and his birth mum) immigration to Canada needed to be put on hold for a while because he had until then not been able to find another job, Queenta quickly jumped to this conclusion in a text message to his cellular phone: "I have always known that you had just wanted me to be babysitting your mother." This is truly a flaviqueenist definition of Momany; implying that the man is a mere schemer or cheater who was never really in love but merely pretending to be, just to use the supposed lover. It is certainly a generalization of Momany as a Bangwa or 99-senser. That was so very disappointing, coming from a woman the man was so determined to spend the rest of his life with, in spite all the opposition within his extended family. Momany found a way therefore to get his biological mum out of Bafut (where she then was residing, also for easy and convenient dressing up of travel and other documents) back to the village before arranging in mid-2008 for an uncle to take her down to Douala while waiting for the materialization of her sponsorship application that Momany initiated in 2010. The Queenta-Momany marriage issue naturally died then, not due to what others had been saying about her but because of the type of person she herself had proven to him to be; which explains Flavie's triumphant entrance in 2009 as the common law spouse.

The Common Law Spouse

Flavie is common law because, at the time, Momany was still legally married to Schola. A Bassa like Anna (but Francophone unlike her), Flavie is the mother of two of Momany's three boys, the other one being from Schola. If Schola has been actively working partially against Momany's objectives, Flavie would seem to have been inactively and completely doing the same. Flavie's case is very pathetic because of two reasons especially. First, she has the advantage of learning and correcting a lot from Momany's experience with Schola who she effectively replaced. This, she has not done, trying instead to foolishly copycat her. Secondly, she has consequently not even succeeded in advancing either herself or the two children she has in Cameroon, to leave out the two boys they have together. It is basically very hard to help a nonoselfist, a person who does not know how or want to help self (Momany's late brother, Dieudonné, and sister, Justine, being other clean and clear cases).

Flavie's case is truly wretched if you imagine that the first gift Momany offered her about a week after their first meeting was the complete kit for learning how to drive (two French books and a bilingual CD), firmly indicating to her: "Just show me your driver's licence and I will show you your car." More than four years later Flavie has never been interested in learning how to drive. You can then tell the rest of the story as far as concerns doing anything that would (and there is practically almost none that does not) involve using a vehicle in Canada. Your understanding of nonoselfism can also be enhanced by Prentice's (2012: 402) analysis of the experiences of Trinidadian workers which reveals the role of emotion, rather than just economic necessity, which draws women into and out of the garment industry. The motivation to learn how to sew, Prentice explains, is driven not by bare economic calculation or necessarily in pursuit of social mobility, but instead can be located in individual projects of self-making. By exploring the role of pleasure in training and performing sewing skills, Prentice's article emphasizes the neglected importance of affect, emotion, and selfhood to understanding economic activity; also showing how the enjoyment which workers derive from learning, sewing, and becoming economic actors is an intimate source of exploitation in the context of waged labour. Nonoselfists would hardly comport themselves like these Trinidadians. Again, Momany sponsored Flavie's *préposée aux bénéficiares* (nursing aid) course in 2009 which she successfully completed and obtained the diploma. Until date she has never worked in the field and worse still does not even know of the whereabouts of her certificate. What kind of person obtains a work permit in Canada and does not know when it expired: unless s/he has never worked with it?

Momany met Flavie at a Cameroonian party in Montréal. She was sitting together with a white guy at a table and many people would have quickly assumed that they were already together and stayed off. Momany is not one of those because (as just seen in Queenta's case) he likes to get that information from the horse's own mouth, not working on assumptions; the doing of which is kind of synonymous to judging B from A's act. As he has himself elucidated on the point, "You simply cannot be true to objectives such as mine if you assume a lot of things. That would mean, for instance, that any man you find sitting at the same table and chatting with your wife is already guilty of adultery." Greeting both persons, therefore, Momany asked the lady if he could sit with her. Her saying there was no problem spelled the end of the other guy's bid.

So, by the time the party hall was swelling with the BMT people,[13] a lot of Schola's 'eyes and ears' at the party would not have believed anyone who would have told them that Momany had met Flavie only that evening in the hall. Was this not looking like reciprocal love at first sight? You could actually read amazement on the faces of the eyes-and-ears especially as they just could not figure out how to get across to Flavie (to do their usual assigned intimidation and blackmail job), not even knowing her in the first place. Momany's friend, James of Gatineau (Québec), told the Flavie 'Surprise and Wonder' Story so well in an email to him on 5 February 2009: "This email is to inform you that we received your letter and the enclosed photo of you and your wife. You have a beautiful wife!! Congratulations! Where did you guys meet? Or did you go to Cameroon for a secret search? She looks fantastic." Yes, James well reflected the feeling that must also have been in the minds of all those "eyes and ears" in the party hall.

Four months later the duo traditionally married in May 2009 in a ceremony that was a "come and see". One of the many things that

---

[13] Listen to Fossungu (2013a: 165) castigating the BMT nonsense: "Is it not purely paradoxical that these people would like... living in the 'Whiteman's country' that is heavily founded on the 'Time is Money' principles but always content themselves with their BMT (Black Man Time)? I find it amazing that most (Black) Africans have decided to immigrate and live in 'the Whiteman's country' but always content themselves with this brainless BMT cover for their gross irresponsibility. Imagine being invited to a ceremony billed for 8 PM. You arrive at 7.55 PM and the hosts themselves are not even ready; and then the occasion ends up beginning at 11 PM, and when you are wondering if your wrist watch had three hours advance and all you get is that 8 PM in BMT is about midnight. What rubbish!"

characterized Momany's Montréal marriage as 'a come and see' (positively unique) is the fact that, for almost the first time, the *B.M. Timers* missed a lot of the wonderful things (traditional African marriage rites) that took place before their arrival, and had to rely on the time-conscious invitees to have an idea of what the time-respecting wedding was like. The time-conscious invitees were doubly happy for the respect they also got from not being endlessly kept there, as usual, waiting for the perpetual latecomers. Momany is known to be of the type of persons that do not start a thing unless they mean to do it well. There was so much hope in the marriage, as evidenced by the number of guests that came from far and wide, by the many praiseworthy speeches made at the event, and by the many "eyes and ears" of Schola that honoured the invitation despite being instructed not to.

But things have simply not been working as envisaged because, like Schola, Flavie also seems to be someone who does not bother about keeping her word. It is not even necessary to get deeply into her general comportment that exhibits a clear absence of any iota of looking at the larger picture. I will limit it only to her own share in the brainless frustration of Momany's attempts to ameliorate the future of the children through uniting all of them by bringing those out of Canada into Montréal. The man has tried his best to make things better for Flavie and the children (the two she had with someone else in Cameroon and the two she has with him). It has simply not been bearing any fruits because it is extremely difficult to help those who do not even know what is important to them or who do not know how to help themselves. Nonoselfism is a hallmark here. There is thus a clear lack of mutual love and understanding in the union.

Worse still and heavily tied to flaviqueenism, even onsilovundism (one-sided love and understanding) would not still be chanced here to bring forth some (*schola-sensical*) successes. For example, the earlier sponsorship for Flavie and the two children in Cameroon, on reaching its final stage in mid 2010, could not go through due to arrears in child support (accrued during the several months Momany was out of work and unable to pay). In 2011, he again undertook to sponsor them as well as Kelie, his first daughter who is still in Cameroon. For all this to happen, Momany had to have eliminated every dime in the arrears of child support to Schola that was still pending. Looking at the larger picture as usual, Momany knew this elimination would take such a long time (if not forever) and the only way through was to have Schola withdraw the issue from the Family Responsibility Office (FRO) and he pays the sum (as per monthly arrangement) directly to her while doing other necessary things such as travelling around and the sponsorships. With Flavie's full knowledge, in November-December 2010 Momany made several trips to London, Ontario, to negotiate the withdrawal deal with Schola who did not want to listen to reason at first. But later she insisted on the deal being notarized (since people who never keep their word always think every other person will do the same), which was done.

In March 2011, the file was no longer with the FRO and Momany put in the sponsorship applications after having made it clear to Flavie that success depended largely on his respecting the agreement with Schola, stressing that the most important thing at the time was for Flavie and the said children to become landed in Canada. This entailed that she had to put in extra efforts in diminishing her nonoselfism and in seeing to it that both of them work hand in hand so that Momany can be able to keep to his engagement to all the parties, including Flavie herself. But, like Scholastica in regard of all the debts Momany contracted in Cameroon[14] and elsewhere to see her through life, Flavie also

---

[14] At the time Schola was studying in the University of Buea (Cameroon) Western Union and other such money transferring agencies were not functional in the country and they had to arrange with Momany's cousin, Inspector Elias, to be providing her with sums of money in emergency situations before Momany could route monies to her on a monthly basis. I am here referring therefore only to the debts they had in Cameroon – one with Inspector Elias (seven hundred and thirteen thousand francs CFA) and the other regarding the arrangements for Schola's coming to Canada via the USA which was contracted through her best

behaved as if the engagement had absolutely nothing to do with her; even being very silly (certainly because of her own scholadela assumption?) to continue exhibiting comportment that unmistakably indicated that, as soon as the trio were landed in Canada, she was going to push Momany deep down into another bottomless hole rather than aiding him to come out of the Schola endless crack. No reciprocal love and understanding existed here as well; and, again, is love without understanding love?

Please, you should all stand up and welcome flaviqueenism into *The Hall of (Definitional) Fame.* Imagine trying on several occasions to reason with someone for her own benefit and all you always get is that you are a dictator. Don't you truly think that (if not the first from the nurse as well), with this particular flaviqueenist description of Momany of all people, flaviqueenism would clearly merit an enviable place in the *Guinness Book of World Records* and in newer versions of dictionaries? Yes, indeed; if Momany, especially, has become one of these tyrants known to Africa especially, there is obviously much that is so very special about flaviqueenism. This Momany-Dictator talk got to an extent that the only sane thing was for Momany to withdraw the sponsorship application; which is what he did (and thank God it had not passed the withdrawal stage!). He had duly informed Flavie beforehand of the withdrawal, and all this notwithstanding how dearly he wanted to help and ameliorate things for the two children tied to her, brother and sister to the two he has with her.

Momany very much loves children, biological to him or not; but it looks like he is never going to have the much cherished chance to give to children (including his biological ones) that ideal loving and caring home with available endless learning opportunities that he

---

friend and Momany's former student in the University of Buea, Edith-Rosa, in the neighbourhood of 4000.00 CAD. When Schola got to Canada she behaved in a way that meant she had nothing to do with these debts, not even those that she herself used to collect from Inspector Elias while filling an exercise book to that effect in her own writing. This book was eventually handed over to Momany when he had fully paid the loan.

himself never quite easily got as a child. He has come to realize that Flavie is an unwarranted un-defining moment to him just as Schola before her, as well as Kelie's mother, Odette, whose odettitooldism is also largely responsible for Kelie not having entered Canada at the same time with Momany in 2002. It as well accounts for the girl (as well as Odette's other children and grandchildren) still not being in Canada to date. You will discover the proper meaning of odettitooldism by finding and meeting that unique woman in this world that refuses a man proposing marriage to her solely because 'I'm too old for you' (Fossungu, 2013a: 160). You can see how a lot of children are not getting what should clearly have been theirs, all thanks largely, inter alia, to the absence of mulovundism, and to scholizyvettism or the calculated use of children as instruments of punishment or enrichment rather than viewing them as persons whose existence in this world resulted from voluntary and reciprocated (and not forced or one-sided 99-sensical) love-making. So, is love without understanding love or just love-making or pretensiousness?

Conclusion

Now that some light has been lit and is shining on the darkness the *apparatchiks* must surely begin to see the issues differently and, hopefully, come out openly. The concerned Africans thus have the choice: they must have to analyse their situation from top to bottom and either keep on doing what they have been doing, or discard even widely held premises whose time has passed [Fossungu, 2013c: 243].

The Folly of 99-Sensism

The lessons of this book are as diversified as the numerous characters interacting with him; but *momanyism*, inter alia, indicates to us that mulovundism or mutual love and understanding would not only be the foundation of any good marital union but also can move mountains that are standing in the way to the formation of that type of union. In most of Momany's relationships examined here there was either much love with little understanding, or both existed but were overwhelmed by outside forces, including both sides of the 99-Sense Theory from fearful and/or scheming parents. Everyone reading has the right to draw the conclusions they see fit. But I can surely not leave you without drawing attention to one of the particularly ridiculous and narrow-minded corners of 99-Sensism. People seem to have 99% Senses but lack the most essential one per cent Sense. Find out for yourself what it is by posing these few basic questions: When 99-sensers keep on selling only cocks (for fear of hens producing for the non-99-sensical buyers), do they ever for one little second think of the day there will be no more cocks available to mate with their many jealously guarded hens? They do scholadelastically-assumed here, don't they? And who, furthermore, would even be the 'buyers' in a world of only 99-sensers? Wouldn't Momany have then become a better or more sensible Bangwa as he has ably theorized at the beginning of this book? Does the world not clearly need its numerous Momanys to be the world, or a better place for all?

As a young man Momany hardly did fit into the definition of family or of child largely because of the 99-sensical home he grew up in. His whole life seems to have been devoted to having an ideal marital union in order to eschew these same problems passing on to his own and other children. But that desire does not seem to be realisable because, as a parent, 99-Sensism and other associated -isms catalogued herein would appear to have trailed him, excluding his ever being included in the definition of family even as a spouse, let alone a mutually loved one. Momany then seems to have learnt a lot on marriage and 99-Sensism from many members of his own large and extended royal family (see Fossungu, 2013a: chapters 5 & 1). But his learning in the fields covered in this book especially did not end with just his extended family.

The Peter of the First Four Women

Outside the family from where he has derived most of the love and understanding survival strategies for counter-balancing the battling 99-sensical forces from both within the household in particular and the extended family in general and the general community, the first four women Momany fell in love with have been very central, each in their own unique way. But one of them unambiguously stands out as the peter or "the rock upon which I have built my love and understanding life and philosophy." Momany is here talking about Annastasia whose use of bolargumentalism rather than the bully's brute force easily liberated him from the one persistent fear (Vincent's knife and yam powers) that would undoubtedly have ruined his life and the objectives he defines himself with. Her intriguing bolargumentalism thus also permitted Momany to learn a lot from her. Fear (as you have undoubtedly seen in some of Momany's siblings' relationships and in Anna's parents) inhibits learning and fruitful dialogue. Might it not also have been Anna's janodilism or fear of her senior sibling that prevented her from confronting Momany in person for a two-way talk during their trying

138

moment in Yoke that ended as a catastrophe? Success with the Ritaian crisebacology that has followed Momany to date is still intimately tied to Annastasia's love and understanding: if you just imagine Momany's life without Rita, with the Kumba school bully winning the physical fight he was then forcing on Momany; envisage his life without Rita, with vincentology still dangerously hanging over Momany in Kumba. Yes, indeed, Rod Stewart sings that *The First Cut Is the Deepest*. I would want to also say *Momany's First Reciprocal Love Is the Most Defining in his Philosophy of Love*, being, moreover, matched with Mutual Understanding.

Liberating and Protecting Momany

Quite apart from the very helpful AAD (Annastasian Automatic Door) that one could somewhat argue is an inborn gift and not necessarily invented by Annastasia, it is obvious that the first two women Momany fell for would not have been able to stand up for him the inspirational way Annastasia did. Miss Mandengue, if she too fell for him as Momany did for her, would have certainly kept the relationship highly secretive; and one doubts that Momany would have accepted its nature, from the way he felt for her. Again, their teacher-pupil status, aggravated also by the age and positional difference, would necessarily fuse into an inescapable fact that should have precluded Miss Mandengue from standing tall (like Annastasia) in front of Mr. Okoro *et al*, if they "caught them" in the Vincent-way. As for Victoria's MTU Girl, doesn't the apparent fact that she must have easily given in to Josephine's threats or other contrivances simply made her inappropriate for the job?

That disqualification of both made way for loving and understanding 'Annasta'. Annastasia not only freed Momany from vincentology but also from those that replaced Vincent. Although Momany learned from his grandpa's stories, Annastasia was the actual invisible hand behind Momany's decisive battle that unambiguously debarred him from becoming another Julie to his two junior brothers of the household (see Fossungu, 2013a: 77-79). Now, imagine Momany's life in the household without the clean and clear

139

victory in that fight. Unlike Sam's senior sister (see *id*: 39-41), Annastasia had mulovundistically demonstrated to Momany that rights are defended and preserved from the very first moment they are threatened. Her two direct junior brothers had initially tried to police her dealings with Momany. She was very swift in asserting herself as their senior and quashing their audacity to want to interfere.[15] Annastasia was very effective and I think it is because most Africans, especially Francophone ones, have failed to grasp this essential lesson that the continent is heavily littered with dictators.

Making Your Own Decision: The Disaster Point

Annastasia also clearly and decisively refused to let Vincent *make her decision for her* as to who she was to date. This is a vital lesson from Momany's first love that has led to disaster every time that he did not rigorously follow and apply it. And this calamity is nowhere more pronounced than in the very spouse arena in which he truly wanted to be far better than his own father. For instance, just imagine Momany's life and the objectives that define it, with Anna as his wife since 1982 if he had not let the Guinness Cameroon manager in Garoua make his decision as to when to go to the University of Yaoundé. Put differently, did the Guinness Cameroon manager then help or mar Momany's future by not giving him the job (as seen in Fossungu, 2013a: 81-82)? That is, would Momany's life be different today and better (or worse) with Anna as his wife (since he would definitely have married her on occupying the post in Guinness Garoua)? Did what thereafter happen in Yaoundé (as seen in *id*: 83-88) a clear way of saying that Momany should not have allowed the Guinness Cameroon manager make *his* decision for him as to when to get to the UNIYAO? If so, did he learn the *decision-making* lesson

---

15 Who then would want to even compare Annastasia's contribution in Momany's life to that of Charlotte (in charalicism): without seeming to be comparing what Fossungu (2013a: 86-88) discusses as the role of the Yaoundé University students who (without food) offered him the train ticket to Douala, with that of the Bangwa man in the American Embassy in Yaoundé who led him to Total Melen and absconded?

well enough (in view particularly of Chantadelamatism)? Also consider Momany's life and objectives if he had not been indecisive in the Chantal-Adela clash in chantadelamatism, thus letting Chantal make *his* decision for him by her 'classy' walking away; and, moreover, this incident also being the only confrontational one of the few times in Momany's life that he sort of flagrantly disobeyed the Annastasian Automatic Door.

Imagine again his life and objectives if Momany had stridently applied the same marriage-decision criterion to Schola who 'has no secret with her father' (Fossungu, 2013a: 152) and backed off as was the usual thing he had done till then – Odilia in chapter 2 above being a clean case. That is exactly how Momany's not listening to Annastasia has led to the re-conceptualization of family that, not only excluded *some types of children* like Momany but, completely excludes him as husband and *all children* (biological or not) of the new definer called Schola. And, finally, imagine Momany's life and where he would have gone so far with his objectives if he had not sort of "chickened out" and allowed tradition decide for him in connection with his cousin who had squarely brought him back into the marriage thing after the Anna-fiasco/Manjo-pregnancy *indecision* leaning towards never marrying. What would Annastasia (one of Momany's greatest ingredients of love and understanding for success) be thinking in this regard? Would another important forgotten lesson from Momany's first and double-virgin love be that Momany had to stick only to a virgin of his for a wife? If that be the case, which of his many virgins (actual and potential) do you think should have been an ideal wife for this atypical **Man Of MANY**?

References

Anyefru, Emmanuel 2013. "The Refusal to Belong: Limits on the Discourse on Anglophone Nationalism in Cameroon" available at http://www.thefreelibrary.com/The+refusal+to+belong%3A+limits+of+the+discourse+on+Anglophone...-a0279891521 [accessed on 11 February 2013]

Avison, William R. And John H. Kunkel, 1992. "Socialization" in James J. Teevan, (ed.), *Introduction to Sociology: A Canadian Focus* (4th ed.) (Scarborough, Ontario: Prentice-Hall Canada Inc.), 55-87.

Beaujot, Roderic, 1992. "Families" in James J. Teevan, (ed.), *Introduction to Sociology: A Canadian Focus* (4th ed.) (Scarborough, Ontario: Prentice-Hall Canada Inc.), 285-327.

Bhattacharjee, Yudhjit 2013. "The Mind of a Con Man." The York Times Magazine online edition (26 April 2013). http://www.nytimes.com/2013/04/28/magazine/diederik-stapels-audacious-academic-fraud.html

Chikkatur, Anita 2013. "Book Review of *Wise and Foolish Virgins: White Women at Work in the Feminized World of Primary School Teaching* by Sally Campbell Gallman (Lantham, MD: Lexington Books 2012) "

Codling, Rosetta, 2013. "Fossungu's *Africans in Canada: Blending Canadian and African Lifestyles?*" available at http://www.examiner.com/review/fossungu-s-africans-canada-blending-canadian-and-african-lifestyles?cid=rss {last visited on 24 September 2013}.

Ferguson, Niall, 2008. *The Ascent of Money – A financial History of the World* (New York: Penguin Press)

Fossungu, Peter Ateh-Afac, 2013a. *Africans in Canada: Blending Canadian and African Lifestyles?* (Bamenda, Cameroon: Langaa RPCIG).

2013b. *Democracy and Human Rights in Africa: The Politics of Collective Participation and Governance in Cameroon* (Bamenda, Cameroon: Langaa RPCIG).

143

2013c. *Understanding Confusion in Africa: The Politics of Multiculturalism and Nation-Building in Cameroon* (Bamenda, Cameroon: Langaa RPCIG).

1998. "Doing Politics without Politics = Lords in Place of Servants" *The Herald* (Cameroon) N° 616 (5-7 June), 10.

1997. "From Peter to Pierre: Même Chose?" *The Herald* (Cameroon) N° 547 (15-16 December), 4.

Gonzalez, Norma, 2001. "Finding the Theory in Practice: Comment on the Hammon-Spindler and Watkins Exchange" 32:3 *Anthropology & Education Quarterly*: 388-392.

Göymen, Korel, 2007. "Interaction of Democracy and Islam in Turkey", in Zoya Hasan (ed.), *Democracy in Muslim Societies: The Asian Experience* (New Delhi: Sage Publicaqtions India Ltd.), 219-255.

Hay, Collin and Daniel Wincott, 1998. "Structure, Agency and Historical Institutionalism" 46:5 *Political Studies*: 951-957.

Hancké, Bob, 2010. "The Challenge of Research Design", in David Marsh and Gerry Stoker (eds.), *Theory and Methods in Political Science* (3rd ed.) (London: Palgrave Macmillan), 232-248.

Jacob, Evelyn, 2001. "The Council on Anthropology and Education as a Crossroad Community: Reflections on Theory-Oriented and Practice-Oriented Research" 32:3 *Anthropology & Education Quarterly*: 266-275.

Ngefac, Aloysius, 2010. "Linguistic Choices in Postcolonial Multilingual Cameroon" 19:3 *Nordic Journal of African Studies*: 149-64.

Orock, Rogers Tabe Egbe, 2005. "The Indigene-Settler Divide, Modernisation and the Land Question: Indications for Social (Dis)order in Cameroon" 14:1 *Nordic Journal of African Studies*: 68-78.

Panky, Wamey, 1997. "Santa Priest Attacks '*Chop Broke Potism*'" *The Post* (Cameroon) (24 October), 8.

Pratt, Nicola Christine, 2007. *Democracy and Authoritarianism in the Arab World* (Boulder, CO: Lynne Rienner Publishing Inc.).

Prentice, Rebecca, 2013. "'No One Ever Showed Me Nothing': Skill and Self-Making among Trinidadian Garment Workers" 43:4 *Anthropology & Education Quarterly*: 400-414.

Rao, Nitya and Munshi Israil Hossain, 2012. "'I Want to Be Respected': Migration, Mobility, and the Construction of Alternate Educational Discourse in Rural Bangladesh" 43:4 *Anthropology & Education Quarterly*: 415-428.

Reaves, Celia S. 1992. *Quantitative Research for the Behavioral Sciences* (Washington, D.C: John Willey & Sons).

Rodrik, Dani, 2010. *The Globalization Paradox – Democracy and the Future of the World Economy* (New York: W.W. Norton,)

Sanders, David, 2010. "Behavioural Analysis" in David Marsh and Gerry Stoker, eds., *Theory and Methods in Political Science (3rd Ed)* (London: Palgrave Macmillan), 23-41.

Stoker, Gerry and David Marsh, 2010. "Introduction" in David Marsh and Gerry Stoker, eds., *Theory and Methods in Political Science (3rd Ed)* (London: Palgrave Macmillan), 1-12.

Watkins, John M. 2001. "Re-Searching Researchers and Teachers: Comment on 'Not Talking Past Each Other'" 32:3 *Anthropology & Education Quarterly*: 379-387.

Weis, Lois and Michelle Fine, 2013. "A Methodological Response from the Field to Douglas Foley: Critical Bifocality and Class Cultural Productions in Anthropology and Education" 44:3 *Anthropology & Education Quarterly*: 222-233.